WHAT HAPPENS IN WAR DOESN'T STAY IN WAR

An Autobiographical Journey through the Stages of Deployment for Family Members, Caregivers and Professionals

Lt Col David F. Tharp, PsyD., M. Div.
Capt Katherine A. Tharp, MD

This is a work of non-fiction. All the events in this book really happened. However, the opinions and interpretations expressed in this book are mine alone and do not reflect those of anyone else. They also do not necessarily reflect the official policy or position of the United States Air Force, Department of Defense, the Department of Veterans Affairs, the US Government, Texas A & M University, Baylor University, Project Healing Heroes, or CombatPTSD.org. These events occurred almost a decade ago, so the conversations in this book are recounted according to the best abilities of my memory. Some details in the book have been changed to respect patient confidentiality. The US Air Force Academy Public Affairs Officer reviewed the manuscript to ensure it did not compromise the security of our military and approved it for publication.

If you or someone you know is experiencing thoughts of suicide, please contact 911 immediately or the suicide hotline at 1-800-273-8255. If you or someone you know is experiencing Post-Traumatic Stress Disorder and are a veteran, contact the Department of Veterans Affairs at 1-800-827-1000. All other symptoms that require immediate attention, please contact 911.

Lt Col David F. Tharp, PsyD, M. Div.
Capt Katherine A. Tharp, MD
Visit the Project Healing Heroes website at www.ProjectHealingHeroes.org

Printed in the United States of America

ISBN- 9781091103054

ABOUT THE AUTHORS: ON A PERSONAL NOTE

LT COL DAVID F. THARP, PSYD, M. DIV., MASW, MA

While in Kandahar, Afghanistan, I was in a NATO billet and served as the medical advisor (MEDAD) to COMKAF (Commander Kandahar Airfield). I was specifically responsible for 28 countries' medical assets. Like most commanders, I had multiple responsibilities and served as the preventative medicine (PREVMED) liaison and environmental engineer (ENVENG). During my tour of duty, I suffered a spinal cord illness that caused me to lose most of the functioning below C2 vertebra. I continued on for another month in that condition, while being treated by a Navy neurologist, until after my tour was complete. I refused to leave, and I was going to finish what I started. In theater, I identified well over 100 service members' remains (probably more, but I didn't really have a desire to count). It was my job to notify the country or the service of the real sacrifice of war. It was then and there that I was changed forever. Thankfully, I went on to recover and continue to serve at the United States Air Force Academy in Colorado Springs, Colorado.

I entered the military as a psychologist after I witnessed on television the attacks on our soil on September 11, 2001. I was so furious from what I saw that I wasn't about to stand by and do nothing. I live by a 16th century quote by Edmund Burke, "Evil triumphs when good men do nothing." That quote alone has impacted my behavior in ways I doubt he could have ever imagined.

After being on the cover of the *Air Force* magazine for an innovative treatment of PTSD in 2008, I decided later on to volunteer for a deployment to Kandahar because I didn't want to be a provider who didn't know what it's like to go to war.

Too many of our providers have the heart to help but simply do not know what it's like. We are trained in military culture and hear the same speeches, but it's very different when you deploy to a war zone, and it's your life that is on the line. I joined to serve and make a difference. While in a war zone, I saw and experienced firsthand the devastating effects of war. I have the deepest respect for our men and women who fight this battle on a continual basis and who experience the full impact of trauma on the psyche and the family. We, the American people, owe them a debt beyond anything we could ever repay. They are willing to sacrifice their lives for this country, and they deserve anything and everything a true servant and warrior should have.

CAPT KATHERINE A. THARP, MD

I was taking pre-med classes, raising two small boys (Joshua, age 4, and Peyton, age 3) and was accepted into medical school at Texas A&M during the middle of David's tour in Afghanistan. I decided to enter the military after living for almost a year with Air Force, Army, Marine, and Navy personnel at Maxwell AFB, Alabama, while David was at Air Command and Staff College. As I lived next door to the families of these brave men and women, I saw firsthand the sacrifice that is made not only by the service member, but by the family members as well. It was then that I decided I wanted to make a difference in their lives.

I chose to serve in the Air Force so that I could use my skills as a physician to help heal those in need, treating the invisible wounds of war. The passion for service, love of country, and sacrifice made by the families, along with the incredible love and support for each other amongst them, was something I had never experienced. My time with them was incredibly enjoyable. I was in awe, and it was then that I decided it was time. Time for me to serve.

(David and Katherine are happily married with two sons, Joshua and Peyton, and reside in Waco, TX.)

***

If you or someone you know is experiencing thoughts of suicide, please contact 911 immediately or the suicide hotline at 800-273-8255. If you or someone you know is a veteran and experiencing Post-Traumatic Stress Disorder, contact the Department of Veterans Affairs at 800-827-1000. All other symptoms that require immediate attention, please contact 911.

INTRODUCTION

So, you want to know what happens when you go to war? Welcome to our attempt to answer that question, and many others. Our goal in this book is to help people understand what it's like to go to war from both a family and warrior perspective. We peek into the world of combat veterans, and what it's like to deploy to a warzone for both the veteran and the family.

Every deployment is different, just as every experience in war is different. However, our hope is that we can accomplish three things by the time you finish reading this book. First, we seek to help the families and caregivers of veterans, as well as medical and mental health professionals, better understand what actually happens on deployment. Second, we lend a voice to those veterans who have a difficult time talking about their experiences. Third, we hope you gain insight into how these experiences can result in a veteran who returns from war very different than when s/he left, perhaps even with Post-Traumatic Stress Disorder (PTSD).

For those of you who either have PTSD or know someone who appears to suffer from the invisible wounds of war, you may wish to consider the book, *The Combat PTS(D) Resiliency and Reintegration Workbook*, available at ProjectHealingHeroes.org. We encourage you to join us in this fight.

For various reasons, many veterans cannot come home from war and talk about their experiences. One of the best quotes I have heard on this topic is from Cameron Dossey who said in an interview, "I don't like people to thank me for my service. There are things I am not proud of. The last couple years I've been stuck in my own head and all I hear is my own thoughts. I tried to commit suicide three times. I never wanted to talk to my parents about what I've seen because in my mind, I'm carrying around the visions of freedom in my head so that they don't have to." [1]

In December 2015, Mr. Dossey attempted to end his life through death by cop. He was so distraught about carrying around these thoughts that at one point he concluded it would be better to be dead than to live with his haunting memories. He was shot by police in Tyler, Texas, and lived. Dossey received psychological treatment in our Resiliency Formation Training (RFT) by Daniel Williams, MD. You can read his poignant and touching story on our website that we created to specifically help veterans with combat trauma. This book illustrates both the sacrifices made by the family and those made by the individuals who not only go to war, but also live in the aftermath. Our hope is to give a voice to those who cannot speak.

When I returned from war like Mr. Dossey, I, too, was reluctant to share any of my experiences because I did not want to adulterate the purity of my family's world back home. I chose to go to war so that America would hopefully not have to deal with the threat of terrorism on our soil. Unfortunately, this has been proven to be wishful thinking.

A direct consequence of deployment is that memories are forever embedded in the brain, specifically in the hippocampus and throughout the cerebral cortex. These are where the long term and consolidated memories that haunt veterans are stored. I wrote an article entitled, "The Away Game," that illustrates why many veterans do not come home and discuss their experiences during a deployment. If you are interested in reading about this, you can find it on our website at ProjectHealingHeroes.org.

After working with hundreds of veterans, it became apparent that a new paradigm for treating veterans with PTSD was needed. I have been trained in most, if not all, of the evidenced-based treatments (EBTs) therapists use, but as a military member who has deployed to war, I have a response to people who write books about PTSD when they have never experienced it. I tell people I'm going to write a book about what it's like to give birth, even though I'm a male. Sure, I can research it and ask hundreds of women to fill out a survey and draw conclusions, but to me,

---

[1] KLTV interview, January 27, 2016.

there is nothing like experiential learning. For combat veterans, war is more than experiential; it's personal.

At one point, I challenged the leading expert of psychiatric treatment in the Air Force about the use of certain treatments on combat veterans. I specifically asked why in the world we would use them, especially since they are based on female sexual trauma survivors. *I argued that sexual trauma is very different than combat trauma.*

His question in response hit at the core of the issue. He asked me point blank, "Well, David, do you have anything better?" I had to respond, "I do not, sir." He said, "Well, when you do, let me know, but for now, this is what we are going to go with; it's all we have." That was ten years ago, and since that time I have taken those comments on as a personal challenge – a challenge not only to deploy to a war zone, but also to do everything I could to understand what it's like to go to war and experience the impact it has on the warrior and the family (including the effects of diagnoses like PTSD) and then formulate an answer about how to treat the issues that result.

The chapters in this book are intentionally short and designed for easy reading. I understand that most people do not have the time to sit down for three hours to read a book. My intent is to help others understand what war is like and how veterans end up in the state we are in.

I thought I was immune to the effects of war. I have a doctorate and three master's degrees, have worked in a Level 1 trauma center, been a hospice chaplain, experienced the loss of both my parents at a fairly young age, and understood on a personal and professional level the trials of loss on the living.

Yet, I wasn't prepared for the impact of war when I stood next to the remains of a 19-year-old soldier covered in a blood-soaked American flag. I watched as the blood dripped methodically to the floor. . . drip, drip, drip. His life, taken from him. At only 19, he was in my eyes a "kid," and he died for our freedom. Like Dossey, I have these memories permanently embedded in my head. No matter how much we desire it, there is no magic pill or memory wipe.

<u>We are forever changed.</u>

Just as with other experiences in life, denial, drugs, or dissociation does not work. Instead, we need to focus on learning from these experiences and find resolution. I am hopeful that in reading this book, you will better understand what actually goes on in the process of war, throughout the deployment cycle from pre-deployment to deployment and finally to post-deployment.

For those of you who do feel broken and see brokenness in the lives of the ones you love, here is an analogy to consider. If you have ever seen the incredible beauty of stained-glass windows, often found in a church, you know that it is impossible to create such a masterpiece without broken and charred glass. As a matter of fact, the more broken the pieces, the more intricate the detail. For some of you, you may even feel shattered. Well, there is good news and hope. We believe that we can help you get your life back. By taking the broken pieces and placing them in the right location with the right mixture of resin that holds it all together, along with rays of sunshine, you, too, can take a shattered life and bring about wholeness and beauty. Instead of just sitting by yourself amidst broken glass, we are asking you to help us bring about healing. You, your loved ones and clients can get better, and I promise, you will never see stained glass or a shattered life in the same way.

The reality is that you would have never seen such beauty had it not been for the shattered pieces we sometimes experience in life. Let's get about the business of bringing healing, kindness and compassion into the lives of combat veterans.

We all go through difficult challenges in life. The question isn't whether they will occur, because they will always occur. It's what you do with them that matters. Unfortunately, people often believe that time heals.

Time does not heal the invisible wounds of war. Ask any Vietnam or World War II veteran. If it did, their issues would be resolved. It's not time that heals – it's what you do with time that matters. Taking the time to read this book and understand what it's like to go to war shows your desire to make a difference. I will tell you that after being to hell and back I began to believe the expression, "YOU CAN'T MAKE THIS STUFF UP," because it proved true over and over again.

Sometimes in the theater of war, things happen that just dumbfound you, but we have a mission to complete, and nothing gets in the way of accomplishing that mission. Our own thoughts and feelings take a back seat to the mission at hand. It's often not until after two to three months after returning home that the "honeymoon" phase of post-deployment fades, and the problems become illuminated. This is when we are in need of the most help.

"THE PROBLEM IS THEY DON'T UNDERSTAND."

I cannot tell you how many times I have heard veterans make the argument that if their family or someone else just understood what they've been through, they would _____
(fill in the blank).

I tell combat veterans the number one rule in therapy is this:

You cannot change other people; you can only change yourself.

I explain it this way. I ask them if they ever think that a person can truly understand what war is like if they have not experienced it? The inevitable answer is "*no.*" Well then, the only way they could truly understand is if they went. So quit trying to make other people understand what war is like, because you can't. They can only understand it if they personally experience it. Instead, I ask veterans to look at what they can do, which is to take care of themselves and focus on what they need to do to get healthy. It is then, and only then, that true positive, healthy changes will occur.

Combat veterans who can accept this basic premise are on their way to becoming healthier. If they cannot, they will continue in their futile state of frustration and bask in its consequences.

As for the family, friends, and providers of combat veterans, I give you this challenge. It's about the heart. If your heart is in it, and you are committed to helping the combat veteran through the issues and challenges, the veteran will do far better. Everyone needs compassion, everyone needs forgiveness, everyone needs a shoulder to lean on, and everyone needs someone to trust. It takes time – time to heal the wounds of war. But it is possible, and you can be successful.

Reading this book and understanding what it's like to go to war is a step toward gaining empathy instead of empty sympathy. And remember, if your heart wasn't in it, you wouldn't have picked up this book. I applaud you for reading this. It shows your heart, your compassion, your resolve to better understand and make things better.

I leave you with two other rules I share with combat veterans no matter how hard it is to accept. After you read them, repeat them at least one time, and let them sink in:

Rule # 1 – People die in war.

Rule # 2 – You can't change Rule #1.

TABLE OF CONTENTS

PRE-DEPLOYMENT

CHAPTER 1: HONEY, I THINK I WANT TO DEPLOY . . . TO AFGHANISTAN

Why in the world would a psychologist who worked for the Department of Veterans Affairs (VA), with two small children at home and a wife in college, volunteer for deployment to Kandahar, Afghanistan? There were two reasons for this, but the most significant one on a personal level was so that I could better understand what our military members go through.

I could either "study" it, or I could experience it. I chose to experience it.

Making the decision to deploy is very difficult. The key word is selflessness. But if you are married and have kids, your focus isn't on you; it's on your family. This leaves combat veterans feeling torn. If you are in the active duty force or are in the Guard or Reserve and get called up, you don't have much choice. We have a word for that, too, it's called "voluntold." On one hand, you want to serve your country, and that is selfless. On the other hand, you are asking your family to carry on without you, which means others must pick up the slack. That is not so selfless, at least on your part. Also, you may feel guilty about leaving, which seems selfish. This is the exact opposite of what you had intended. This internal struggle is what I call "deployment guilt." It's a simple definition but a complex emotion: it is the guilt one feels about deploying. You feel both national pride and sacrificial desire to serve our country while at the same time you feel horribly guilty for leaving your loved ones.

When I deployed, I thought it would be the very last time I would see my wife's grandmother. She was 102 at the time. When I returned, she was 103 and just kept on ticking. But trust me, the guilt was still there, especially with my immediate family. My wife had a lot of responsibility when I left. She was pre-med, working part-time, and taking care of our house and our two young sons, Joshua (age 4) and Peyton (age 3).

She struggled with wanting to support her husband while also knowing the demands placed on her while I was deployed would be intense. This is why I believe it is often harder for the immediate family than it is for the person deployed because it is they who pay the bigger price when it comes to deployment. If you have a family, it can be very overwhelming to know they will have to continue to meet the demands of your home life minus you as an asset. It's like having a weak link in a chain. But instead of being weak, it's entirely removed. Even with all the guilt and thoughts weighing on our minds, my wife and I decided it was time for me to deploy, and she graciously and gladly (at least most of the time) took on the extra responsibility. Little did she know the toll it would take, but we would soon find out.

CHAPTER 2: THE VA NEEDS YOUR ORDERS . . . YEAH, WELL SO DO I!

There is a reason the military calls them orders and not suggestions. REPORT! You never wonder where you stand with orders. You stand exactly where they tell you to stand. If your orders say Kandahar, you're going to Kandahar. So when I told my employer, the VA, that I was headed to Kandahar, I was asked the logical question: "May I please have a copy of your orders?"

I replied, "Certainly, when the Air Force gives them to me."

The VA let me know that once it got them it could release me. It was all good -- well, except for one small detail.

The Air Force told me that I wouldn't have orders soon enough, but that if I were to go on this deployment, I needed to report that next Monday at the Air Force Academy. What the military doesn't quite understand is that there are too many former military personnel working for the VA, and they know better. So, it's a no-go until you get the orders. I told my VA human resources person that I had to report on Monday. Their response of course was that they needed a copy of my orders.

This deployment was not starting out the way I thought it would. I couldn't get orders. The VA wouldn't release me until I had them. It was a Friday afternoon, and I needed to report on Monday. Yeah, this was going to be a fun deployment. Just a small glitch in the system, right?

It eventually all got straightened out with a VOCO, Vocal Orders of the Commander. They're not regular orders; they are verbal orders . . .that are then written. Don't even ask why they don't call them WOCO, Written Orders of the Commander, because that would make logical sense.

CHAPTER 3: SAYING GOODBYE TO FAMILY – GUT WRENCHING

Gut wrenching. Those are the only words I can think of to describe it. Sure, I could wax more eloquently, but the reality is, it hurts. It hurt right smack in the gut. I don't know how people who deploy multiple times do it. (Although if things continue as they are, it won't be long until I know exactly how that feels.) Honestly, they are amazing folks because they have willingly given up what they love most: family and freedom. I have heard it said that when you join the military, you are signing a blank check over to the US government, including, but not limited to, the cost of your life. It's no wonder why less than one percent of the US population is willing to serve. I almost called this book, "The Less Than One Percenters."

There is a significant, positive, correlation between the gut-wrenching pain one experiences and the love one has for one's family. Let me say it another way: the more you love your family, the more it hurts. I hated it. We seldom use the word hate in our family because it carries such a strong connotation. God hates sin. Well, I HATED leaving.

My wife is amazing, she truly is. Most people think their spouse is beautiful, smart, patient, kindhearted, generous, loving, including all of the fruits of the spirit. My wife really is those things. While I am writing this, she finished medical school at Texas A&M College of Medicine and is currently in residency at Baylor Scott and White in Temple, Texas.

I have two amazing, cute, adorable, sweet little boys for whom I would lay down my life at any moment. There's a saying we often use in our family, "I love you so much I would die for you." I've lately challenged them to say instead, "I love you so much I would live or die for you." If going to Kandahar was a possible death sentence – which, by the way. . . well, we will get to that – I was willing to pay that price any day of the week, especially if it meant that the people of the United States, and specifically my family, would be protected from terrorism.

Even though I had two small children, there was a time in my life I never thought I would be that lucky. I had been married before. My first wife and I were not able to conceive for medical reasons. In my whole life, I never imagined going through a divorce, but it happened. I thank God that I found myself happily remarried with kids. I distinctly remember telling Katherine that I would love to be married, have two children, and all the financial stress that would entail. What a foolish man I was for the financial stress statement!

Knowing I was about to deploy made every second with my family precious. *Every second.* I knew I needed to spend as much quality time with my family as I could, despite all the preparatory things that needed to be done around the house before I left. I would stop and just love on them – kiss them, hug them, and stare at their beautiful faces because I knew I didn't have much time left with them. I worried that the time I did have with them could be my last on earth. I wasn't trying to be dramatic, but this was on my mind. Deployment really changes one's perspective – it did mine before I had even left.

We have another saying in our family: people are more important than things. But when you aren't going to be there to get the things done, it's a worry. So, I tried hard to have the boys with me at all times whenever I was working around the house getting things ready. They got to have fun with Dad, learning new things, and we got to spend time together. I still do this. It is truly a joy for me . . . most of the time.

As this was my first deployment to a war zone, I had lots of questions burning in my brain. What if this is the last time I get to spend time with my family? What if something happens to me, and I don't make it back? What if God allows me to sacrifice for my country, and my kids have to grow up without me as their dad?

I remember my father telling me that his father died when he was just five years old. I saw the impact that this has had on him throughout the years. Five was almost the same age as my oldest son Joshua. I just took another punch to the gut thinking about the impact not growing up with a father made on my own dad. We, the Tharps, are resilient. My dad taught me to never, ever, under any circumstances, quit. I never will. It's something I want to pass on to my own children.

Minding my father's advice wasn't always easy. In high school, I was under 5 feet tall and weighed in at 98 pounds. Yet despite this, I wanted to play football because my brothers did. I even had to go to junior high youth football just so I could get a helmet that would fit. My head was so small the high school helmet spun around on my head. Ah, the memories.

The thoughts kept coming. What if something does happen to me? Will my kids remember me? How will they remember me? What if God truly allows the unthinkable to happen? Tears would roll down my face when I thought about these things, but I made sure no one ever saw them. That all changed the day I was to leave.

Trying to explain to your children who are in the concrete operational stage of development[2] that you are leaving for a year is very difficult. It wasn't that long ago that they learned the secret behind peek-a-boo (object permanence - even though my hands are hiding my face, it's still there). Joshua, at only 4 years old, had the hardest time understanding that I was leaving for that amount of time. To tell you the truth, at three years old, I don't think Peyton even had a clue. I could leave for a long weekend

---

[2] The concrete operational stage of development means that they see things literally, not abstractly.

due to military responsibilities, come back home, and Peyton would act as if I had never left. Joshua had a harder time with my being gone. All I could think of was, *"how do I prepare my kids for deployment, especially the fact that Daddy won't be here for an entire year?"*

We decided to celebrate Joshua's birthday early, just so I could enjoy it with him. The kids asked me if I could take them to birthday parties and told me what they wanted for Christmas. We talked about things they wanted to do, but I knew in the back of my mind I would be deployed.

You can tell children you are leaving, but it's not in their cognitive makeup at this stage to "get it." My wife often had to remind me by saying, "David, they are three and four years old, just give it up." But I wanted them to know how much I loved them, so I constantly told them, "I love you as far as the East is from the West." Peyton has since learned a new word – infinity. He often asks, "Daddy, does God love us infinity?" "Yes, Peyton," was always my reply. "And I love you as far as the East is from the West." Then he would ask, "Daddy, which one is longer, infinity or as far as the East is to the West?" You gotta love kids!

I remember thinking that this deployment may kill me, not physically, but emotionally.

The day arrived, and I had packed up everything I thought I would need. I spent the whole weekend on the internet researching what to take on deployment. For example, I would need 550 cord. I didn't even know what 550 cord was. It seemed it was highly coveted on deployment and could be used for almost anything: hanging clothes, tying things together, pulling loads, etc. I was starting to feel like MacGyver – that guy portrayed on television who could get himself out of any situation with just a toothpick.

It was time. We finally made it to the Waco airport, and, I swear, gut wrenching is the understatement of the century. Having to say goodbye to my family tore my heart out. I explained to my kids that Daddy was going to be gone for a long time, but that I was coming back. All the while I knew this would be the only lie I had ever told my kids if I died and didn't come back. It ripped my heart out when I thought about it. *Dear God, please do not let that happen*, was a prayer I prayed often. I needed to somehow find comfort in the process of assuring my wife that everything would be fine and in telling my kids I would return. God is that comfort for me. He is a very big help in a time of trouble. I leaned on God a lot during that time. People say there are no atheists in foxholes. I hadn't even left home, and I felt as emotionally vulnerable as if I were in a foxhole.

Between thinking about deployment and getting my bags together, time seems to get away from you. The plane was at the gate. I was leaving out of Waco, Texas, and heading to Dallas, then off to the Air Force Academy in Colorado Springs. I was an Individual Mobilization Augmentee (IMA) – others call it I aM Alone. Literally, you are a onesie. You deploy by yourself without support staff, no brothers in arms, no comrades, no one. Just you. I guess that was a benefit of being a psychologist, that I could go it alone. In reality, it's a horrible way to deploy. I have since become a person who dislikes it very, very, much.

Over the loud speaker I heard, "This is your final boarding call for flight 193, please proceed to Gate 1." In Waco, Gate 1 is easy because there is only one outbound gate. Sometimes I think they say that just for fun. It was my turn, time to go. I looked at my wife, and with tears threatening to spill from my eyes, I gave her the biggest and most intense hug I could without breaking her ribs.

Joshua asked, "Daddy, why are you crying?"

I replied, "Because sweetheart, I'm going away for a long time, and I miss you guys already." By now, my tears were falling to the ground.

Joshua held my hand, looked up at me, and said, "It's okay, Daddy, we love you." This still brings tears to my eyes. It hurt horribly. I hated it with everything I had. I didn't want to go. I wanted to stay home. I HATE THIS! I've made a mistake. Let someone else go in my place.

Time stood still. I know I did. I had a sense of being in another world; I didn't want to face reality. Here I was, this psychologist who had it "all together." *WHATEVER.* I hated it, and I didn't want to leave. That's all there was to it.

We said our goodbyes, and I got in as many hugs and kisses as possible when we heard the call to board. My house is only about two miles from the airport as the crow flies, and I knew I'd be able to see it when the plane flew over.

It was time for Katherine and the boys to leave. "I love you guys," I said. "I'll be gone for a long time, but don't forget me. Be good for Mommy, and know I love you as far as the East is from the West."

I went through security and off to Gate 1. That is when they left. It was probably better that way. Seeing them through Plexiglas for possibly the last time brought me no comfort.

As I sat there waiting to board the plane, I realized I hadn't felt that much pain since my father and mother passed away. Yet still nothing was as hard as saying goodbye to my wife and kids. I have been through hell, almost died three times, performed the funeral for both my parents, seen death firsthand in Level 1 trauma centers, but this, *this* was harder. It was so much harder. I looked down at my phone (a flip phone my wife made fun of me for having) and thought, what would happen if I called and told them to come back? I just want to see them one last time! No, I couldn't. It was hard enough. I had to let go.

Just a few seconds later, I heard an announcement, "Well, folks, Flight 193 to Dallas has been cancelled due to mechanical failure. The next flight out is Monday morning. We will rebook you, if you desire."

WHAT? I *had* to be in Colorado Springs on Monday. The military said so! I only had five days to prepare for deployment, something that normally takes three weeks. I could not wait. Now what would I do?

I quickly dialed Katherine. I told her that I knew it sounded crazy but the flight to Dallas was cancelled. I only had two hours until my next flight left out of DFW, and it is one and a half hours to Dallas. Did she think she and the boys could drive me? She was so excited and couldn't wait to say "YES!"

When she and the boys pulled up, Joshua, in full concrete operational mode said, "Wow, Daddy, you are home already. That didn't take long." Oh, Joshua, if you only knew.

CHAPTER 4: AIR FORCE ACADEMY, HERE I COME

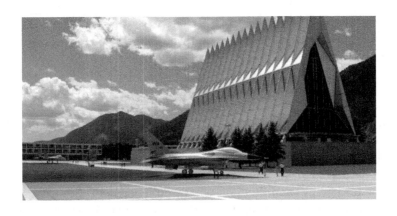

Once I finally received my VOCO, I was off to the Air Force (AF) Academy. The AF Academy is beautiful: fresh air, mountains, and the spirit of the AF Academy itself. It was exhilarating to be there, but at the same time, it was emotionally numbing. I tried to wrap my mind around being away from my family for that long, and it was depressing. Numbing is a healthy way to deal with some of the pain because your other option is to be overwhelmed with emotions. I started to understand why numbing is healthy, at least for the time being. I also understood why numbing is a defense mechanism.

Time was definitely not my friend. For this deployment, we needed to get all three weeks of training completed in just five days. Yes, only five days! Oh, did I mention the VOCO didn't include a car rental. The AF Academy is not a small base and trying to get all of my prerequisites for deployment was daunting. After four hours of trying to figure it out, I finally got the VOCO from headquarters for authorization of a car. Neither headquarters nor I had thought about that tiny detail. There went four hours of my five days of training that I wouldn't get back.

Military members have heard many, many times the phrase "Hurry up, and wait." This experience was the epitome of it. The military is very insistent on ensuring you have every possible vaccination known to man. I swear they gave me more vaccines in one day than I've had in my entire life. On top of that, they drew so much blood, I actually passed out. If you've never had that wonderful experience, I'll describe it for you. All of a sudden you cannot hear anyone talking, the room gets very narrow, your peripheral vision gets narrower and narrower until – BAM – you hit the floor. Yeah, that's what it's like, loads of fun. If it's any consolation, at least you don't feel it when you hit the floor. But, boy, do you get a lot of attention when that happens.

After 14- to 16-hour days trying to get all my requirements in for medical, dental, vaccines, gear, weapons, food, orders, more shots, more gear, (yeah, you've got it), I was exhausted. Then it was time to go back to the hotel. Just a small piece of advice: NEVER, EVER, EVER spray DEET on your military clothing INSIDE your hotel room. Yes, I did just that. It was a huge mistake. I'm sure I killed a few lung cells with that decision.

On a positive note, the AF Academy was playing a home football game that weekend, and I wasn't heading to Fort Dix until Monday. Football is a nice distraction. We won. Distraction, better known in its more amplified version as avoidance, versus dealing with pain, was a concept I could live with. Avoidance is one of the criterion in the Diagnostic and Statistical Manual 5th edition where Post Traumatic Stress Disorder is defined, but what would that have to do with me?

CHAPTER 5: WELCOME TO FT. DIX, AND "IT'S PIZZA DELIVERY TIME . . . FOR INSURGENTS"

Have you ever wondered whether you could be killed by terrorists inside a US base prior to deployment? That is something I never imagined I would have to think about or deal with. Yet, it was the top news story a few weeks before my arrival at Fort Dix. Two men dressed as pizza delivery guys tried to get into Fort Dix with the intention of killing as many service members as possible. Their plan was thwarted only because some savvy guy who was printing their photos notified the authorities that something wasn't right. For the first time, I was beginning to understand Maslow's hierarchy of needs and why safety and security are at the base of his pyramid. Without those two things, not much else matters. I realized my life was now going to be in danger. I was going to war. I hadn't thought about how that would impact me. I still remember the feelings as if I were experiencing them today.

I was in a new place, toting 300 pounds of gear that was impossible to lug through the airport without leaving one of the pieces unattended. How was I going to get all that gear from one place to another in the Baltimore airport at 2 a.m. when there were no carts, no one around, and I was worried that if I left even one bag behind I'd be seen as a terrorist dropping off a bomb? Also, I wasn't wearing a uniform as was military policy for fear of being targeted. I really had no choice but to leave one bag behind while I dragged the others 75 yards and then went back for the remaining bag. It was very frustrating. But God is in control, right?

When your life is threatened or you perceive it to be threatened and your safety and security are in jeopardy, you naturally find things that give you security. Mine is in God. When all else fails, when others leave you, when your parents have died, when there is no one left, God is there. I'm so thankful to my parents for raising me in a Christian home. I cannot fathom how people do this without feeling a sense of comfort, security, and confidence knowing God is right there with them. I wasn't even really in danger, but I was praying a lot more. I guess this is normal.

As for training, well, let's just say the Army will kill you, even before you get to Kandahar. I had not been as exhausted since high school football two-a-days, and that was 28 years ago. There are reasons 45-year-old men should not go to war. Even though I felt really strong, and was in great shape, my stamina was NOT what it used to be. Thankfully, through incredibly thorough training, the military makes sure you are prepared. One of the key things you get is a lot of up-training in the military. What you don't get is a lot of down-training.

Some of our trainers had actually just gotten out of the military and were working for a contracting company back to the US Army. These guys were hard core. They yelled at us repeatedly, warning us that the enemy would kill us if we didn't listen to them. I realized these guys were for real when we were training with paintball guns, and they actually hit me in the groin and in my shooting finger within five seconds of saying, "Training begin!" Now that's some skill. I couldn't even pull the trigger because my finger hurt so badly. We won't even discuss the groin issue. Reality check: I was preparing for war.

DEPLOYMENT

CHAPTER 6: ROTATOR – IS THAT A HELICOPTER?

Honestly, I didn't even know what a rotator was, but I sure wasn't going to tell anyone. In the military, there are natural rivalries between the military branches of service. Rivalry increases e*sprit de corps*. However, in the Air Force, and especially the reserves compared to the active duty force, there is a belief that we don't know what we are doing. Partly this is because many of us in the reserves do this part time, not full time, like the active duty members. So when it comes to acronyms and other things, we simply aren't as well versed. Most civilians are also not familiar with the language, acronyms, and culture. This contributes to the disconnect between the military and civilians.

Many of the active duty guys and gals had been deployed three or four times already, and they weren't even 30 years old. So, I learned to be very good at situational awareness through observation. The rotator, by the way, is how you get in and out of theater. Theater is, of course, not a place you go to see a Shakespeare play, but a war zone. That seemed simple enough. You often take a commercial flight to some European country and from there start boarding military aircraft. In case you haven't had the pleasure, let me tell you – military aircraft do not have noise reduction systems or insulation. They are loud, and they are cold. Thankfully, I had brought a pair of noise reducing headphones. Some of my research had actually paid off. These headphones reduced the noise, but they did not eliminate it. There is a BIG difference. So not only could I hear the "white noise," but I could also hear everything else while I froze.

The C-17 Globemaster is a pretty awesome airframe. It's relied on heavily to get a lot of people in and out of theater. When we left for Georgia (the country, not the state), I quickly came to appreciate people of higher rank and the fact that we are a North Atlantic Treaty Organization (NATO) asset. Welcome to a NATO world in a NATO war. The Georgians are amazing folks who have been at war for a LONG time. They deserve their own chapter.

CHAPTER 7: GEORGIANS AND WEAPONS

After four days of very little sleep, hurry up and wait, and leaving the comforts of the US, we finally landed in Tbilisi, Georgia. After waiting four hours for the Georgians to get on the plane, we sat there, and sat there, and sat there, and then sat there some more. Another four hours went by. Then I heard it, "Who is the SRO on this plane?" When I finally got the courage to ask the guy next to me what an SRO was, he looked at me, looked at my rank, and sighed, "It's the Senior Ranking Officer." I got the very clear feeling I should have known that. Man, was I glad that I was only a major. Finally, a US Army colonel stepped up, and it was clear a conference was about to take place. But first, we clearly needed an interpreter to ensure proper communication. So, we waited, and waited. Two hours later the command came: everyone deplane. This is when you don't ask questions; you just do as you are told.

We got off the plane and were told to make sure we did not have any ammunition on us. I wondered who in their right mind would bring ammunition and a weapon on a plane, especially after 9/11. Our weapons were already stowed underneath the plane in the holding area, so I was a bit confused. After a few more hours of waiting and then re-planing, we found out what happened. Apparently, while the Georgians had no problem having weapons and ammunition on board a plane, the US Air Force had a different take on this issue. Clearly, the Georgians wanted to go into theater with weapons and ammo. The US thought this was a bad idea. Much later in my deployment, the Georgian physician whom I commanded and I were talking about the issue we experienced in Tbilisi, and he asked me, "So what will you do if your plane goes down and you have no ammunition or weapons - throw your canteen at the enemy?" I prefer the Georgian way of thinking.

CHAPTER 8: WELCOME TO KANDAHAR – "YOU CAN'T MAKE THIS STUFF UP"

Welcome to Kandahar Airfield, better known as KAF. Anyone familiar with KAF quickly equates it with Poo Pond. The Poo Pond was literally a pool of feces in the middle of the base where all the raw sewage was collected and "recycled." What was initially designed to handle 4,000 people was now overflowing from the need to accommodate a base that had grown to over 30,000. Poo Pond was built by the Russians in 1972 on the outside of the base. As KAF grew, and because the base had limited space, over time the city built up around Poo Pond. So this particular scenic attraction, once on the outskirts of town, was now right smack in the middle of KAF.

In the picture above, Poo Pond is the distinct circle that looks like a pie cut into four equal pieces. Today, the pond is completely surrounded by military personnel.

When I arrived at KAF, utterly exhausted from the eight-hour long, freezing cold flight, which landed on the world's busiest single runway, I slowly gathered all 300 pounds of my gear and threw it into a corner. Unlike at a major airport where there is a concierge or someone from one of the airlines whom you can ask for guidance, there was no one. We all stood there wondering what to do. After about half an hour, a Marine approached and asked, "Are you Major David Tharp?" It's possible he figured that out because my rank is visible, and my name was clearly written on my uniform, although only my last name, so I figured this guy knew for whom he was looking.

I acknowledged that I was, and he motioned me to go with him. Please understand, even when you outrank someone, when they are 6'5, built like a Mack truck, and have a chiseled face, you proceed accordingly. I followed him, thinking, well, if nothing else, this guy certainly should be able to handle any Taliban we meet along the way.

We grabbed what I thought was all my gear and started the long walk to the Humvee. We headed out to the Entry Control Points (ECPs). As we drove around to the first ECP, my new Marine friend asked me if I had any questions. I said I didn't, and we moved on to the next one. After about 10 minutes of driving through dust and austere landscape, we arrived at the next ECP. Once again, I observed the high lookout tower occupied by military personnel with machine guns facing outward. I thought they were M-16s but later learned they were M-4s because they have a shorter stock and can be maneuvered more easily, especially in confined spaces, such as a Mine-Resistant Ambush Protected (MRAP) vehicle.

What was interesting was that these were not US personnel. I don't know, I kind of expected them to be all US, but then this was a NATO base.

My Marine friend asked again whether I had any questions about the ECP. When I again replied with a no, he seemed a bit agitated. So, being the brilliant psychologist that I am (that's a joke), I began to wonder why the heck this guy was driving me around and asking me about ECPs. Was he trying to orient me to the base? Was he showing me how protected we were? Maybe he was trying to help me gain a grasp of the other nationalities we were working with? I had no idea. After another 15 minutes, we reached the outskirts of the base, and he pulled up to a third

ECP. We got out, walked around, and he said, "Major, do you have any questions?" This time his voice changed and he was clearly wondering why I didn't have a single question. I had finally reached my limit as well.

"May I ask why in the world you are driving me around to all of these, whatever you call them, ECPs?" I asked.

"You are Major David Tharp, correct?" he asked.

"Yes," I responded.

"Well, from what I understand, you are our new Force Protection guy at KAF."

WHAT? Stunned and confused, I remembered during my research that less than four months earlier the Taliban had taken a tractor, blown a hole through the fence, and created a breach so they could, let's just say, do some real damage. I also remembered hearing that the Bulgarians were not allowed to shoot unless they were being shot at, so there they were, standing armed and ready but unable to shoot while the Taliban breached our fence. I remembered it took a Canadian Quick Reaction Force (QRF – yay, I remembered an acronym!) to take control and annihilate the enemy. Thank God that they didn't have the same Rules of Engagement on firing their weapons that the Bulgarians had!

While all this was going through my mind, the Marine was waiting for my response. Dust was blowing in our faces, and I could smell Poo Pond. All I could think was, "what the heck? I'm not Force Protection! I'm a psychologist! You want me to be Force Protection? Are you crazy?"

But I thought it best to be proactive instead of reactive so instead of expressing those thoughts, I said, "By the way, did you grab my gun?" (I later learned I should have called it a weapon.)

He looked at me with unconcealed disgust and said, "No, that's your responsibility."

"I thought you got it," I said. "Where the heck is it?" We had to go back to the hanger (which I later found out is called the TLS – Taliban's

Last Stand – of all things). No weapon in sight. Oh great, less than an hour into Kandahar, and I'd already lost my gun, um, make that my weapon.

I looked at him and shrugged my shoulders. He responded with a very frustrated look and said, "You are NOT going to be our Force Protection guy!"

"Good," I responded, "now that we've solved that issue, take me to the general so I can do my job." All the while I was smiling on the inside because I'd just escaped the first unofficial job I was about to be forced into doing. Oh yeah, I thought I was pretty smart with that one.

We finally took all my stuff to the TLS headquarters where I met a British soldier who was the Executive Officer (XO) for Brigadier Moulds, British Armed Forces. He was the man in charge at KAF. I don't think I had ever met a Brit before. Nice chap, if I do say so myself. From my history class, all I could think was, "darn good thing we won the war; otherwise, you would be speaking with a German accent." (Please, no offense to my Brit friends, they are truly awesome and a godsend.)

I finally got to meet BG Moulds, but he didn't have much time for me. A quick handshake, "Welcome chap," and off he went. I figured he was a pretty busy guy, prosecuting a war and all. I wondered where my friend Lieutenant Colonel (Lt Col) Jordan was. I asked my new Marine friend if I could get a ride to billeting.

"Dude, you're not FP (Force Protection), you are on your own. Find it yourself," he said with a glare. I guessed we wouldn't be best friends after all.

The TLS was a mess after being burned, shot at, and bombed. There was a huge hole in the middle of the TLS where we'd purportedly set off a five-hundred-pound JDAM (a big bomb) but didn't set the fuse. The Taliban were occupying it, and we just wanted them to know we could have blown them up if we wanted. But heck, we built the TLS back in 1960 for $5 million, so we sure weren't going to blow it up.

Someone asked me if I had seen all of the bullet holes in the five-foot thick concrete? Ah, my new home. Can't wait. He told me that if I looked up behind the wall prior to the huge crater in the roof, there are gingerbread men off to the side. Later when I asked about this, I found out that each gingerbread man represented ten Taliban we killed during the fight for KAF. There were over a hundred of them. I can only imagine the fighting that took place to take control of the TLS. How many men got killed on our side? What a price for a runway. And yet it's now the world's busiest single runway, so clearly it had significance to the war. Its location is central to Regional Command (RC) South. I desperately wanted to climb up there like a tourist and see those gingerbread men but thought twice about it when I realized how difficult it would be to explain what I was doing. Plus, I had already lost my weapon. I wondered what I was going to do if the Taliban attacked. I'd better find that thing, I thought. The good news at least was that I still had my M-9, so that brought me some comfort.

After dragging my stuff four blocks to the small trailer where billeting was, I discovered it was closed. Oh, great! This place smells and there is no one at the inn. All I could think of was, "I hope I'm not in one of those tents." I was thinking like an entitled person, but honestly, I knew what that would mean. I just didn't want to do it. I was very tired, and I just wanted to go to sleep. Although after a while, even a tent looked good.

After several hours just hanging out, watching people run in the dust, and trying my best not to choke on the smell and dust from the MRAP vehicles driving up and down the street, I finally found the person in charge. I got my room key (yay, no tent) and headed up the dirt road. Oh, good, I was rooming with a Brit, my favorite people. Brits were only one of three nationalities I had met that day, and I couldn't speak whatever the Romanians were speaking (possibly Romanian). I felt as if I were back in college and wished I had taken a few more foreign languages.

I was missing my wife terribly, and I'd left my two small children so that I could better understand what people who serve go through in war. Whose idea was that anyway? Oh yeah, mine.

In the morning, I finally made my way back to the TLS where I was supposed to start my new job, whatever that was. I only knew it wouldn't be Force Protection. When I reported, I discovered that everyone knew about the psychologist who lost his weapon. Dang, I'd thought I could hide that one. I had no such luck. I didn't have any ammunition, so what was I going to do, throw the gun – oops, weapon – at them? You know, I work hard to break stereotypes about mental health professionals and how reservists are viewed. Clearly, I hadn't started off by making a good argument against the prevailing opinion at this point in my deployment.

So, I'm a trained psychologist. I have plenty of education, and I'm ready for some psychological issues: people who have PTSD, depression, anxiety, insomnia, you name it. I am ready for this psychological challenge!

I get my assignment. I'm the MEDAD. What is that? MEDAD stands for medical advisor. "But, sir," I said to the general, "I didn't go to medical school."

"That's okay, we are NATO, close enough," he replied. Close enough? No, NOT close enough! You need a physician, not a psychologist. Isn't there someone on this base who went to medical school? The general continued the conversation that I will paraphrase to the best of my recollection: "Oh, by the way, you are in charge of 28 countries here, many of them require an interpreter. There is no consistent computer system because everyone uses their own, we have a phone system but it's complicated, and most people don't use it. I have a guy who's been covering that job, but he's leaving tomorrow and wants to get out ASAP. You will definitely be his new best friend. So you might want to meet with him, get the scoop, and get to work."

This was crazy. I was in the middle of a war, stuck at the TLS, doing a job meant for a physician, and I did not speak any other languages. I knew I should have taken German or French in high school! I was feeling very unprepared. So much for my Boy Scout days of being prepared at all costs.

It was time to meet my new best friend. That's what you are called when you come in to replace someone. Why? Because my presence meant he could get the heck out of Dodge, or in this case,

34

Kandahar. I met with this very fit gentleman, also named David. Cool, I thought, we both have the same name. A very nice chap; yeah, a Brit. I thought he was on speed. Honestly, the guy talked incessantly. He drew on white boards faster than I could blink and went through things so quickly I had NO idea what he was talking about . . . MIRP, Role 3, Role 2, Role 1, FOB, COB, birds, PREV MED, ENV ENG . . . I was totally lost. "Can you go over that again?" I asked.

He looked at me and said "Nope, I have to pack. You'll figure it out in time, just like I did," and promptly left. That was the last I saw of him.

At this point, I was very seriously wondering if I could go home. I'd changed my mind – I did not want to be there. I just wanted to be like all the other researchers and clinicians and read about it. It would be a lot safer. I wouldn't be feeling totally lost or exhausted. I wouldn't be missing my family so terribly. I wouldn't be eating dust all day, working in a building with bare wires everywhere, looking at bullet holes in the wall, seeing where residue from the fire that killed the Taliban had reached the ceilings, and I wouldn't be in danger! Reading about it was starting to sound like a great idea. Most professionals never join the military; they enjoy the benefits of making money, staying home, and enjoying the good life.

I was feeling a bit of resentment coming on – and regret.

When I first arrived in Kandahar, I was a little awestruck about being a NATO asset and who would be my boss. I had seen the new brigadier general (BG) who was taking the place of the departing Brit. He was US and Air Force and had just arrived at KAF.

I was a little intimidated. I wanted to make a good impression, and I really pride myself on being successful in whatever I do. I was amazed to see my friend, LTC Jordan, eating with him at the Dining Facility (DFAC). He waved me over and introduced me to Brigadier General Jeffrey B. Kendall. He was sitting down eating but still very intimidating with that star on his shoulder. Thankfully, he has a very contagious smile. He was both polite and incredibly welcoming. I was still in awe and a little nervous, but he made me feel very comfortable. Before long, we were joking around, talking about the Air Force Academy where he graduated and where I worked. We talked about family and other topics. What a great guy.

The next week, I discovered I would be working with him directly and thought, "Yikes! I really hope I do a good job." After all I have done in my life, you would think I wouldn't be so intimidated or nervous but, alas, I was.

Let me set the stage for our first trip to the Afghan market.

The location for the market is actually on KAF. The locals bring their sellable items to KAF and set up shop. I was invited by LTC Jordan to accompany him and BG Kendall, and although I hadn't yet acquired any cash, I wasn't going to let that opportunity go by. So, off we went in his car with his security folks and chauffeur, an Air Force Second Lieutenant. Going through security checkpoints, even on KAF, is a LOT easier with the general. He is the highest commanding officer and is called COMKAF (Commander, Kandahar Airfield) for a reason.

It was fun looking at all the things the Afghans had to sell. They have beautiful stoneware that is carved and polished to perfection. I loved it so much, I thought about how in the world I would get that home. As we were walking around, it was clear that people respect rank. Thank God that you do not salute in a war zone, because we would never have gotten anywhere. Otherwise, my right arm would look like Popeye making my left arm look pretty puny.

Folks are so accustomed to saluting that we often had to remind them not to salute. The theory behind not saluting in a war zone is that doing so identifies the person being saluted as a higher-ranking officer and makes them an easier target. As we walked around, the Afghans were very friendly, smiled all the time, and clearly did not have many dentists in the country. Ah, another thing I love about the US. We stopped at a little "shop" that was more like a flea market stall than anything. The Afghan businessman was selling beautifully made rugs. The detail was exquisite, and again I thought, "how in the world would I ship that home?" It was evident that there had to be a way, because I watched several service men and women buy items. I later learned that they usually wait until they are close to going home before purchasing them, and that made a lot of sense. I had just arrived, so I guessed I should be patient about buying things.

While we were standing there looking at the rugs, one of the rugs started to fall. In that split second, and without thinking, I used a very unfortunate word. I said, "Incoming." Yup, that was what came out of my mouth, and before I could blink, everyone had hit the ground except for the BG's security force, who released their safety locks, took positions, weapons up-range, and scanned the crowd for threats. Except for me and the Force Protection (FP) guys (who I was supposed to command), everyone, including the BG, was on the ground. The dust flew up, and I was left standing there. In Kandahar, you'd think it was sand, but honestly, I think it's more like moon dust. I gained situational awareness while everyone else was on the ground. You got it, just me and FP, now unlocked and loaded, were standing. Oh, my gosh. I couldn't believe I had just said that.

Of course, there was no incoming rocket. I later learned that rockets came in 3-4 times a day. After a few seconds of hearing nothing, the BG, who was still on the ground, turned over, looked up at me, and said, "Tharp, what did you see?"

"Well, sir," I said hesitantly, "It was a . . . uh . . . a rug."

"A *what?*"

"A rug, sir. I saw a rug falling." He looked at me incredulously but quickly realized how embarrassed I was. I said, "I think I used a really unfortunate word, sir."

"You think?" he said. Then with a smile, he said, "Major Tharp, you are going to clean my uniforms this whole tour." Surely, my face was crimson. LTC Jordan just looked at me like, *What were you thinking?* Honestly, I was more afraid of his security staff who were all glaring at me. I didn't say another word for the rest of the day. All of his staff, however, enjoyed making fun of me. It certainly wasn't a short-lived joke for them.

For the Air Force folks reading this, all I can do is ask for forgiveness. I did not represent us well in the beginning, but it will get better, I promise.

This was one of my first experiences with the BG, and I wanted to crawl under a rock. Why in the world did I have to choose *that* word? I can assure you that I never used it again. So much for making a good impression. LTC Jordan and I did get a good laugh over it later.

That was just the beginning of a great relationship with the BG. He could have really made my life horrible, but he laughed it off. That set the stage for the rest of our tour. He truly is an amazing leader and an amazing man – a godly man who truly believes in taking care of his people – and I have the utmost respect for him. I would do anything for him, even clean his uniform – which he didn't actually allow me to do.

CHAPTER 9: WHAT DO YOU MEAN THEY CANCELLED MY ORDERS? DOES THIS MEAN I GET TO GO HOME?

KEESLER AIR FORCE BASE
81ˢᵀ TRAINING WING
OFFICE OF THE BASE COMMANDER
228 377 2179 DSN 597 2179

12 September 1972

To: All Kessler Base Occupants
Subject: Interruption of Gravity - Civil Engineering
Compliance Work

On 0900 Saturday 16 September the 81ˢᵀ Civil Engineering
Squadron will be instituting structural renovations to all
barracks to ensure their compliance with AFS standard 72-
47c-31d. These renovations will require lifting all
Unaccompanied Enlisted Personnel Housing off of their
foundations and adding structural cross members to ensure
their compliance with above cited AFS standard. The
attached base map lists the affected barracks.

Orders cancelled

To ex_____rily
interrupt gravity from 0900 to 1600 for construction access
under these barracks.

Only the campus areas south and west of Base Drive will be
affected.

Civil Engineering has advised that the interruption will
create non-causal gravitational singularities along the
boundaries of the region affected. Therefore Hurricane
Drive and Base Drive will be closed to traffic throughout
the day.

All personnel are advised that the following precautions
must be taken:

1. Officers with families and those in Bachelor Officer
   Quarters may leave the base before 0845. Take all pets
   including waterborne animals.

2. Due to danger of walking outside, all enlisted
   personnel are confined to quarters 0845 to 1615.
   Barracks leaders will sound the All Clear when normal

I had prayed and asked God to allow me to experience everything that military members go through during deployment so that when I saw veterans in the VA system, I could not only relate, but also *empathetically* relate. Bad idea for a prayer. God takes prayers seriously, you know.

So, there I was, three weeks into my tour in Kandahar, and I got a message from headquarters. "Major Tharp, your orders have been cancelled." What? I was confused. Were they kidding? How? What did that mean? Was I leaving?

Had I actually thought people didn't experience craziness from even our own military service in a war zone? I mean, if executing a war wasn't challenging enough, let's just cancel the man's orders, shall we? I finally discovered that this was a mistake, but what wasn't quite as funny was when I was told, "Um, Major Tharp, you're not getting paid either." Now that was *not* funny.

My wife and family count on me to provide financially for them. It's not like I could jump on a plane and get back to work in a matter of hours . . . or could I? Was I supposed to just go home? As it turned out, it wasn't that I wouldn't be paid at all, I just wouldn't be getting a paycheck in two weeks. It was going to take six weeks. Were they kidding me? Even though it was a small stressor, it was the beginning of a long, stressful tour of duty.

In dealing with PTSD, people think it's one index trauma. They can't be further from the truth. It's not one; it's a hundred. It's not like getting shot. Deployment is like getting cut a hundred times. The stress never stops on deployment. It comes in various forms with the best of all being rockets and indirect and direct fire. Welcome to the S in PTSD.

CHAPTER 10: TECHNOLOGY AND BEING
HALFWAY AROUND THE WORLD

Joshua talking to me on YouTube, age 4

Kandahar felt as if it was exactly halfway around the world to me. There is an 11.5-hour time difference between Kandahar and my home in Texas, which created some logistical nightmares. I had been apart from my wife on many occasions due to military drill, but not to that degree. Maintaining a relationship from that far away is difficult without technological challenges, but when you add in that dimension, it's a whole new world. We had intermittent internet in Kandahar if you were willing to pay $100 a month. Skype was wonderful – when it worked. I think I spent most of my time in Kandahar watching a frozen screenshot because the bandwidth was so poor. But I wasn't about to complain, at least I could hear my family. You are appreciative of what you get when you don't have things, and what you thought was important really isn't any longer. *This is how one's baseline begins to change.* Remember that last point because it becomes vitally important in dealing with military members when they come back home.

On one particular night when I was Skyping with my wife, KAF got hit by a rocket attack. I tried to remain calm and said, "Well, honey, I have to get back to work. Time for me to go." I prayed she hadn't heard the explosion. This was the benefit and downfall of technology. Psychologically, I sometimes

Peyton talking to me on YouTube, age 3

think it would have been better not to have technology at our fingertips. I cannot even begin to tell you the number of times I felt guilty about not being home to keep things running smoothly.

On one occasion, my wife and I were Skyping, and she told me that the pool filter had broken, and she was trying to use a "C" clamp to get it to work. Unfortunately, her remedy wasn't quite working as she had hoped, and without the filter running, the pool would begin to turn green from algae in no time. My wife was doing a fantastic job, but again, it's akin to becoming a single parent with two kids. The job at home didn't stop; the house had its own set of challenges. The pool needed to be cleaned and repaired, things broke, she was in school, and the kids needed and wanted their daddy back. It was an emotional nightmare at times. But know this: even though these things were on my mind at the time, what was in front of me took precedence. This is very normal in a combat zone.

What was even worse was when one of my friends/buddies/wingmen/soldiers got killed. It was incredibly hard not to post on social media sites what we were dealing with and how this had affected me. But we were constantly told not to do so, partly so that the family of the deceased could be properly notified and also because of the need to not give any information to the enemy. Unfortunately, not everyone followed this order, and it definitely created psychological stress for many families of fallen soldiers.

In a situation where you need to maintain the ability to compartmentalize your feelings in order to continue doing your job, there must be an emotional outlet in theater. I found this in praying and in spending time in the United Service Organization (USO).

One of the benefits of the USO was it had much faster internet, computer, and Skyping capabilities. This was a blessing for those soldiers, sailors, airmen, and Marines who couldn't afford the $100 a month or were on maneuvers and, thus, weren't stationed at the same location. The USO was a godsend in what seems like a godforsaken land. The only problem was when you have a good thing, everyone wants to use it, which is why the MWR (Morale, Welfare and Recreation)[3] and the USO were always packed. I could finally communicate with my family, but I was a few feet away from another guy who also wanted to talk with his family. Privacy was nearly impossible.

People did their best to respect other people's privacy for the most part. And honestly, you will sacrifice anything to talk with your family. Psychologically, the challenge was trying to maintain some sort of compartmentalization. If I fell apart, I wasn't keeping up with my job. And not to do my job was not an option. People rely on each other. Most people handle this fairly well, but when a friend is killed, that's a whole different issue. You learn not only to compartmentalize, but also to keep things inside.

We all hear it time and time again, "pain is weakness leaving the body." So where does that leave us in regards to emotional pain? You learn to stuff it. Plus, I didn't want my loved ones to know I was having a hard time. I was tough; I could take it. Big boys don't cry. So as my deployment went on, I learned to keep my emotions to myself. I had a job to do, and I could not afford not to do it. Maybe, I thought, I'd get to figure out how I felt about it later. But later didn't come, because there just wasn't time and, the truth is, it was discouraged. I was starting to understand why people keep things inside. It's a sign of strength. I wondered if this was why my father didn't share what he went through in the Second World War, or why my brother didn't share about his experiences in Vietnam.

---

[3] An MWR is a physical place where military members go to make phone calls, get sports equipment, play games, etc.

But I didn't have time to think about that too long. I had a job to do. It was back to work.

CHAPTER 11: WE HAVE MANY BENEFITS FOR YOU WHILE YOU ARE AWAY AND WHEN YOU RETURN HOME. OKAY, NOT REALLY.

There truly are some amazing benefits for deployed service members and their families, and for that, we service members are very appreciative. The problem is if you actually have a need, chances are that others do as well.

The YMCA is a wonderful organization that has done a tremendous amount of good. I have the utmost respect for the YMCA, and it has been there for many families in need, both military and civilian. I believe in the YMCA's core values of care of mind, spirit, and body. So, it was a natural fit for the Department of Defense (DOD) to pair up with the YMCA to support America's warfighters. With the government's involvement, though, comes governmental complications.

The YMCA had a program that allowed families of military members deployed to a war zone to join for free. Did I say free? Nothing is free – don't you remember your father telling you that?

My wife was doing her due diligence, trying to obtain all the prerequisites she needed to increase her chances of getting into medical school while also managing our house and taking care of our two boys. We all know how the challenges of family and school can mean that fitness often falls by the wayside. Being a loving husband, I recommended she take advantage of this wonderful DOD agreement with the YMCA and hit the gym, not only to increase her physical health, but her mental health as well. As a psychologist, I am well aware of the mental benefits of exercise. I actually wrote part of the Fit to Fight program for the US Air Force and spoke on this subject at the American Military Surgeons of the United States (AMSUS) conference.

My wife contacted the YMCA, told them of her interest, and set up an appointment. She took the forms required, filled them out, and returned them. Two weeks later she grabbed her yoga pants, went to the gym and was informed they didn't have her paperwork. Confused, she replied that she dropped the paperwork off two weeks previously.

They repeated that they didn't have it. She calmly asked to fill out the forms again. They gave her another set of forms which she filled out. Upon returning a third time, she was then told we were "ineligible." This wasn't exactly the kind of support you hope for when your husband is deployed to a war zone, and you are trying to take advantage of something healthy for yourself. So using my checkbox system, we tried to figure out EXACTLY what the problem was, and what box we hadn't checked.

- Military member – check.
- Paperwork – check.
- Spouse deployed – check.
- DOD/YMCA agreement in place – check.
- YMCA availability – check.
- Desire to exercise – check.

So, what was the problem?

It turns out when you are a reservist you have to be deployed for at least six months. Well, I was deployed for at least six months. Actually, I was away from my family for over 10 months. So what checkbox did we miss? Apparently because the YMCA lost the initial paperwork, by the time they processed the second set of forms, I had just five and a half months remaining in Kandahar. Why is this important? The checkbox for the six-month requirement was marked: INELIGIBLE.

Are you kidding me? I was in a war zone, fighting for my country, but because the paperwork got screwed up (and not by us), my family couldn't enjoy a promised benefit? Most military family members that are active duty have a gym on their base, and most Air Force Reservists who deploy to a war zone go for six months (make that 179 days so we are denied more benefits), and you jack with my family over this? It would be better not to tell people you have something for them than to promise benefits and then deny them.

So, what did I do? I contacted the Pentagon from Kandahar. I explained the situation, asked for guidance, and after three days of "I have no idea," my persistence paid off. (My parents would say my stubbornness paid off.) I finally got a response.

"Yes, you are correct, Major Tharp. You are now ineligible," was what I was told by the Pentagon official in charge of the benefit.

"You MUST be kidding me!" was my not-too-happy response while rockets were going off outside.

"I'm afraid so," I was told. "We only have so much money and we cannot offer this unless you have a six-month tour."

"But I do. Look at my orders!"

"Negative sir. You technically have five months and two weeks left." This might give you an idea of where the condition trichotillomania could have originated. It's a condition where you pull your hair out. I was dealing with the Pentagon, and I wanted to literally pull my hair out.

CHAPTER 12: CONFIDENTIALITY IN THEATER

There are many times I've found my role as a psychologist and a minister very challenging. One thing I definitely lost when wearing my psychologist hat versus my chaplain hat was confidentiality. Both maintain confidentiality, but if someone reports to me as a psychologist that they want to kill themselves or others, I have a legal obligation to break confidentiality and intervene. As a chaplain, I do not have the same legal obligation, although I may have a moral one. I would much rather wear the chaplain hat than the psychologist hat at times. It gives me more options. Plus, people will often not speak with a psychologist because of stigma involved. In addition, chaplains are not afraid to discuss spiritual issues, whereas many psychologists come from a more liberal perspective that often does not integrate spirituality into the mental health realm – at least in the mainstream.

As a psychologist, it wasn't surprising to me that I deployed as something other than a psychologist. At a time when we needed this type of specialized personnel, I didn't even deploy as a provider. As a reservist, one of the challenges is being credentialed. I could spend my two weeks a year getting credentialed, or I could actually do my job as a psychologist at the Air Force Academy and see cadets. So, unfortunately, I wasn't credentialed as a psychologist for the Air Force. Instead, I became the medical advisor and a psychological consultant to the Army. I fully expected to be dealing with family issues, psychological issues, some theological challenges, sexual assault, TBI, PTSD, etc. Well, that did happen, but there were a lot more significant things that occurred for which I was not prepared.

On one occasion, without breaking confidentiality, I was confronted with the following scenario:

I had a female soldier who was having serious difficulties with her commander. He made her life extremely difficult by making her feel incompetent, creating internal feelings in her that she wasn't doing her job (which I knew she was because I had seen her in action), telling her he wanted to demote her, and perpetrating all sorts of psychological warfare on her. Finally, after months and months of trying to appease him, of going through chain of command and getting no relief, she ended up becoming suicidal and coming to me as the consultant.

She knew I had connections at the ROLE 3 (the main combat support hospital on KAF that housed our Level 1 trauma center) and could get her the help she needed, and she knew I was a psychologist. Coming to me wasn't manipulative on her part; it was strategic. She desperately needed help, and she knew I wouldn't turn her away. I helped coordinate at 2:00 a.m. – make that 0200 – a contact at the ROLE 3. After almost an hour, we were able to see a social worker. I quickly learned that when it comes to this type of emotional trauma, it's best to kindly provide guidance to young troops who are doing their very best, but are just that – young and inexperienced. So after some time, and with some guidance, the social worker was able to at least ask the right questions.

Finally, after reviewing her notes and telling the soldier that she would consult with her supervisor in the morning, she told this soldier that there was really nothing she could do with the situation. They were useless to her. Out of sheer intense frustration and fear, this woman cried profusely and said she felt suicidal. I needed her to tell the counselor, and she did. Again, after another hour (it was now about 0600), the counselor told her that she was sorry, but there just wasn't anything she could do. She told the soldier that she could possibly get her some medication, but she had no jurisdiction over the situation. The only way she could do anything was if her commander was being sexually inappropriate with her.

I heard the bell go off in this soldier's head. "Why yes, yes he has been," she said. I could tell by her demeanor that this was simply not true. But again, she was being strategic. If she couldn't find any relief through chain of command, through her commander doing the right thing, or through becoming suicidal, she decided the only avenue she had for getting out of her situation was through the legal authority the medical personnel had regarding military sexual trauma (MST). So, she took it. Does this mean every person who wants out of a bad situation will take whatever avenue they can? I don't know. I only know she was offered a golden ticket . . . and she took it.

Because the situation wasn't dealt with correctly, we now had an MST situation. I say situation because she and I both knew she hadn't experienced MST. This creates a serious dilemma for headquarters when it comes to a very important issue. It also creates problems for commanders and for the troops when it comes to morale, appropriateness, integrity, chain of command, etc. I do not fault her, but in my opinion, it was not the right avenue to take. When someone's safety – even their emotional safety – is threatened, they will do what they have to do to survive.

CHAPTER 13: FIRST EXPERIENCE OF DEATH: AN ARMY SOLDIER AND AN AMERICAN FLAG

I had been in theater probably about three weeks, had settled into my new job as the MEDAD, and was trying to come up with systems that worked, all while we were receiving incoming indirect fire (IDF) rocket attacks. Our response time was roughly 22 minutes, and that was way too long for me. The base wasn't even that big. The problem was that the Brits had their own system of doing things, and the person in charge of the security teams was, to say the least, inflexible. On numerous occasions, I stopped by to discuss with him some courses of action (COAs). Each time, my ideas for decreasing our response time were dismissed. Being strategic myself, I decided a different plan of attack was in order because clearly repeating myself and using logic was not working. I knew flexibility was key. After all, flexibility is the key to airpower, so why not deploy that same line of thinking here?

My direct boss at the time was another Brit equivalent in rank to this gentleman, and the good thing for me was that they disdained each other. This worked to my advantage on a few occasions. Eventually, I read in the NATO regulations that I was supposed to report directly to COMKAF because they did not want a mediator between the MEDAD and the COMKAF. When I brought this up after another medical incident, my boss was supportive and even recommended it. I proceeded and got it changed. Then the unthinkable happened.

It was late at night when another rocket attack occurred. Standard procedure for COMKAF staff, as well as all other military personnel during a rocket attack, is first to hit the ground to avoid getting hit with the explosive or shrapnel, wait two minutes in case of another attack, and then respond accordingly. Everyone else on base was to head to the nearest shelter. On the other hand, COMKAF and his entourage headed to the TLS to create our response to the attack. That night was the first night it hit me. It wasn't shrapnel; it was a proverbial ton of bricks.

After I responded to the IDF and went to the TLS, I headed over to the ROLE 3 to identify any military members who had been injured or killed. The initial reports are almost always wrong. If it says 15 injured, it's three. If it says two killed, it's ten – it's just the nature of the confusion. It's called the fog of war. I always reminded BG Kendall about this, even though he was probably thinking, "I know that David, I've been around a lot longer than you." Still, he was always kind, patient, and helpful. He trusted me. But I only trusted my own eyes, especially because the information would constantly change. That night we were told of one injury. BG Kendall told me not to worry about it, to head back to the NATO barracks, and we would pick it up in the morning. Something internally told me otherwise. I told him that with all due respect, I'd like to follow this through until the end.

He concurred and appreciated my follow-up. He told me to just brief him in the morning, unless he needed to be awakened. This was always his response. He trusted my judgment, and I loved that about him.

After seeing my friends at the ROLE 3, it was normal for me to head to the Tactical Operations Center (TOC). I verified the situation but was briefed that the information was incorrect. What a shock.

I was told I might want to check with the surgeon on this one because it was "pretty bad." It's about a 20-foot walk across the trauma bay, so I did just that. "Hey, Major Tharp, you made it over quick," was the surgeon's response.

I laughed and replied: "Yeah, well, I laid on the ground for about thirty minutes just to make sure there weren't any more rockets coming in." Of course, we were supposed to stay down for just two minutes. We both laughed. Then his eyes dropped. I'm trained in Neuro Linguistic Programming as a psychologist, but honestly, anyone who has any knowledge at all knows this isn't a cognitive response but rather an emotional response.

"This one's pretty gory," he said. "You may want to identify from the neck down."

I thought that was a strange thing for a surgeon to say. In hindsight, I know he was trying to protect me. He knew my job, and he knew I could get the name of the soldier off his uniform. I could read the patches and figure out what country and division he was in. From there, with his ID, I could most likely make contact with the Army across the street and get the notifications going. Tonight was different, though – very different.

This one stopped me in my tracks. It actually stopped my breathing. The trauma bay is usually one of two things: VERY hectic or very quiet. It was *very* quiet. One of the nurses took me over to where the soldier's body lay and said, "He's over here, sir." I wasn't prepared for what I saw next.

An American flag was draped over his entire body. It was completely blood soaked. I had never seen a flag draped over a body before, let alone in this condition. The blood was dripping from the corner of the flag onto the floor in a rhythmic drip, drip, drip. It didn't even seem as if the blood was clotting. The trauma team had done their best to save him, but they knew it was a lost cause. "He suffered a head injury, sir," the nurse said. "You may not want to see it; it's pretty bad."

"It's okay, ma'am," I responded, even though I outranked her.

"Do you want me to take off the flag, or just pull it back for you?" she asked.

"I can do it. It's okay. You must be tired. Carry on," I said. My breathing became slow and shallow. Actually, very slow, so much that I could feel my chest rise and fall within my uniform. I knew this guy had breathed his last breath barely 15 or 20 minutes ago. I didn't want to proceed too quickly, or even at all. I stood there, staring at the blood-soaked flag. It was shaped to the outline of his body. His boots were still on. I reached over and took his hand. It was still warm. I prayed, and cried. Time seemed to stop. As the tears welled in my eyes, I could only stand there frozen. I looked over every inch of the flag and his body. This was somebody's son, a brother, a friend. I knew he probably wasn't even 21 years old. He wasn't married, or at least there was no ring on his finger. He laced those boots up. He volunteered to come join the fight. He wanted to make a difference, and yet here he was. Halfway around the world, dead. His family didn't even know yet that he was not alive.

All I could think of at the time was the poor family. Then it hit me. Even though it isn't supposed to be about me, it hit me like a proverbial ton of bricks. The questions flew through my mind as I stood there in total silence. What if *I* die? What if I don't make it out of here? What if the last time I saw my children was just that, the last time. Will I ever see my wife again? Will I ever see my family back in Illinois again? What if this were me lying there?

As a chaplain previously, I had dealt with a lot of death. That's what happens when you work in hospice. Death was not new to me. I did not fear it, but what I did fear was what it would mean for my family. It would mean my kids growing up without a dad, and my wife having to go on without me. My sister, whom I dearly love, would be crushed. I thought about my brothers, and how they would each respond. Time stood still. I'm sure that it had only been a few seconds in real time, but it seemed like eternity. Oh God, where are you? Where are you right now? Where were you when this man got hit? Is he a believer? Is he now in heaven? Why did he have to die? Is this all for naught?

That night was the first night I realized I truly was in a war zone. My breathing hadn't changed; it was still shallow. I could literally feel the air through my nostrils as I breathed and my chest rose and fell. I choked back the tears, and it was then I realized I was still stroking this man's hand. The warmth made me realize how close he was to having been alive. Then the nurse came over and put her arm around me. "Major Tharp, are you okay?" she asked. Honestly, it took me a while to respond. Initially, I couldn't speak. I just looked into her eyes with tears in my own, and nodded up and down, my chin quivering. I couldn't stop blinking, I think mostly to make my eyes quit crying. It didn't work.

"Yes, ma'am," I finally managed to say. "Yes, ma'am," was all she needed to hear. I actually thanked her, and we gave each other a hug. All I could think at that moment was that this was a horrible war. Then my brain went to a place it had never been. I realized: *This is a war, and I'm in it. This is real.* My heart sank. Reality had hit home for me. I was in a war zone. This wasn't all training and preparation. This was real.

I took my hand and pulled the cover back and saw that more than half his head was gone. Now I understood why the flag had so much blood in it. I stared and cried. I had never experienced such deep respect for anyone as I did for him that night.

This kid, this soldier, made the ultimate sacrifice for our country. He cared enough to give his life. And what have we given him?

CHAPTER 14: THE USO AND ITS AMAZING IMPACT

Truly, the USO is a godsend. What an amazing group of people, an amazing resource for those of us in a war zone, and a reprieve from the reality of war... I have never met as many dedicated people as those who serve for the USO.[4] What first stands out is that the Kandahar USO is like an oasis in an otherwise nearly colorless landscape. In Kandahar, you mostly get beige and army green. The USO was very different. Every wall was painted a different color, covering the spectrum of the rainbow. They had televisions, computers, telephones to call home, video games, greeting cards to mail home, and, on special days, food that people had shipped from the United States. I could tell this wasn't their first war.

There is truly no way to adequately express how this little USO oasis was like a refreshing cup of cold water – especially given how hot Kandahar can get. Whenever I could volunteer for the USO, I took advantage of the opportunity. It was an honor and a pleasure to serve alongside the USO staff members because it clearly made a difference in the lives of so many soldiers, sailors, airmen, and Marines. They created every

---

[4] People like Sarah Kemp, Erin Mintmier, and Randi Moresi Baker

game imaginable to keep us motivated and help us forget about the war, even if for only an hour or two. I distinctly remember a game I had never seen before. It was called Beer Pong, and the USO was hosting a tournament on St. Patrick's Day. You could say I was a bit sheltered. I had not chosen to participate in a few time-honored college rituals. I was like, "So all you have to do is get the ping-pong ball in the cup?" Heck, I can do that. There were 10 teams, and low and behold, I discovered I have pretty good hand-eye coordination. My partner and I kept beating each team we came up against, and in the final match, I nailed the last shot. We won!

Yes, that's me in the Beer Pong challenge. After celebrating our win, I reported to work the next morning, and BG Kendall and I were talking. He asked why I seemed so upbeat and happy. I told him that he wouldn't believe what I got to do last night. I said excitedly,  "There is this game called Beer Pong that I'd never heard of, and it was a blast. We had so much fun at the USO, and I wished he could have been there."

To put this into context, you have to understand that General Order 1B in the military states there will be no, I repeat *no*, alcohol in a theater of

 war. You can imagine BG Kendall's face as I was sharing my great news with him and going on about how I thought this was such an awesome game. I even showed him pictures of all the fun we were having. He

listened quietly, a look of disbelief and then dismay growing on his face. He said kindly, "David, you know you can't drink alcohol in theater. What were you thinking?" He was looking at me as if I'd just told him, the *general*, that I'd spent the previous night getting sloshed. And I had pictures to prove it! He must have been thinking, what am I supposed to do now?

It finally dawned on me. "Oh, General, I'm so sorry, I should have clarified. It was root beer! I don't even drink alcohol."

You should have seen the relief on his face, knowing he wasn't going to have to remove me from duty and give me an Article 15. I should have known by then how important it is to be very careful about what you say in a theater of war. You'd think I would have learned that after my "incoming" misadventure. Because I don't drink alcohol, I didn't even think about the implications of the game's name. It's not my frame of reference. One thing is certain, when you are in a war zone, your frame of reference changes dramatically. If you learn nothing from this book, make that a takeaway. **Your frame of reference to things changes dramatically**!

I just loved working for BG Kendall, and I can only imagine that he had to shake his head a few times when he thought about me. But you build great friendships in theater, and it was nice to work for someone as relaxed as he was. Otherwise, I might be writing this book while sitting in the brig!

This is the type of fun the USO brings to theater. It's a wonderful experience, wonderful people, and a wonderful organization. I cannot say enough good things about the USO and the people who work for the organization. You really have to be there and see people finally able to drop their guard, their situational awareness, their hyper-vigilance, and relax for a few hours watching TV, playing video games, talking with their families over VOIP (computer telephones), to be able to appreciate the contribution the USO makes. I loved being able to grab a birthday card or a "thinking of you" card for my family and send it to them. There isn't enough time or room in this book to fully explain the impact people like Sarah Kemp, Erin Mintmier, Eric Raum, and Randy Moresi Baker made in my life and in the lives of hundreds of other military folks. This is the one place where certain people in America put their values to work and reach out in a tangible way. THANK YOU!

As a matter of fact, it was Raum and Moresi Baker who created a video while in Kandahar, Afghanistan, that went viral. You can see it here: http://abcnews.go.com/Entertainment/making-hit-marine-call-video-afghanistan/story?id=16809981

CHAPTER 15: THE MILLION DOLLAR BIRDS

Given that KAF is the world's busiest single runway, there is one natural enemy that fighter jets and others have to deal with: BIRDS. The last thing a pilot wants is to fly through a flock of birds and have them shut down an engine (or two). There are all kinds of devices designed to keep birds away from the runway – everything from noisemakers to owls to sonic boom guns. At KAF, we had a problem with birds. The birds were smart enough to nest in one of the very large hangars down from the airstrip, and there were hundreds of them. I became aware of this situation when our flight safety officer dropped the problem in my lap.

"And how is this a medical issue?" I asked.

"Well, there are birds, and therefore bird poop on things, and we don't want to have any birds infecting people with their poop." He must have seen by my expression that I thought this was a bit of a stretch. He added, "Well, the birds can fly into the intake of a jet and put the pilot and others at risk. They are human pilots, so that's in your lane." I just shook my head, and we laughed.

Personally, I thought his first argument was more creative. Anyway, it fell into my lap, and I had to come up with a plan. The general was well versed in what can happen to an airplane when it flies into a flock of birds, and he wanted to ensure we did not have an aircraft mishap that could hurt or kill a pilot and passengers, or shut down our runway. So, what did our NATO allies recommend we do to solve the problem? Get a contract to have the birds captured or exterminated.

I talked with the NATO Maintenance and Supply Agency (NAMSA) about what it would take to eradicate the problem. We put out a request to fix the problem and received a proposal to the tune of $1 million. NAMSA's idea was to put up a net that would capture the birds and also a net to stop them from nesting in the rafters. I asked the question, "if we do this, which I could imagine we needed to, what would stop more birds from going into another hangar?" The answer was simple: *nothing.* You've gotta love the honesty. I could not see us paying a million dollars for every hanger to keep the birds out of KAF. There were probably 15 or more hangars. That would be a very expensive solution.

The flight safety officer and I got together and talked about getting into the bird eradication business. I wasn't going to go this alone, especially because he had made this my problem. After our laugh about the cost and wanting to make a million dollars off NAMSA with our own contract, we seriously had to come up with some COAs for the general.

It is customary to present a senior ranking officer with no fewer than three COAs. We presented the million-dollar solution, then a second solution that involved a fake owl meant to scare off the birds (although the effectiveness of this owl had not been verified), and finally the third and winning COA: we bought a pellet gun and let each military member have 10 shots to see how many birds they could kill. By the end of the month, we had eradicated every bird in the hangar. We should have gotten a medal for saving the US and NATO a million dollars!

It really worked. The "sharpshooters" honed their skills, we eliminated all of the birds so we wouldn't have some kind of epidemic on our hands (again, my responsibility), and I was able to report that the situation had been mitigated. I doubt the general would have chosen that particular solution in another setting, but it was efficient, effective, and done at a considerable cost–savings, with the bonus of boosting morale. We solved the problem. What more could you ask for? Oh, right, a medal.

CHAPTER 16: PTSD FIRST HAND

At the time of my deployment, I was a clinical and research psychologist at the Veterans Integrated Service Network (VISN) 17 Center of Excellence for Research on Returning War Veterans and, more importantly, a psychologist both for the VA and the Air Force. I was trained and well versed in the signs and symptoms of PTSD. To wind down after a typical 16-hour day, I often made my way to the USO to try to decompress, all the while hoping I wouldn't have to respond to IDF, and also hoping I'd get at least a few uninterrupted hours of sleep. Sometimes when you are that exhausted, you don't really want to talk with people, but neither do you want to be alone. If you allow your job to consume you, it certainly doesn't make for an enjoyable tour of duty.

Most people in the civilian world change out of their work clothes when they go out to enjoy some relaxation. On a deployment, you are in a military uniform 24/7. Military members do not get to change into civilian clothes and feel normal in the AOR. By this point in my tour, I didn't even remember what civilian clothes felt like. So one evening, as per usual, I headed down to the USO. I said hello to the USO staff and sat down to enjoy watching one of the televisions they have there. This is what I and others normally did if we were waiting for a computer to become available, or waiting to get access to a telephone to call the US. You'd put your name on the list and wait.

On this particular day, I encountered a soldier who epitomized what PTSD truly is. This soldier was approximately 20 years old. I do not recall his rank, but clearly, he was pretty new in his career. He sat there, almost lifeless, with that thousand-yard stare we sometimes see. Although I was exhausted, and the last thing I wanted to do was to start a conversation, there was something about him that tugged at my heart. I had come halfway around the world to better understand what our military goes through, so I couldn't let a little exhaustion stop me. But believe me, I was tempted.

I said hello, and either he didn't hear me or, most likely, was dissociating (a psychological term meaning detached from your surroundings). I sat there and thought about whether to engage or not. Maybe I should just relax, wait for my computer time, and rest. I shook my  head back and forth, trying to motivate myself and shake some of my fatigue, and decided to re-engage. "Hi, I'm Major Tharp. What's your name, soldier?"

He blinked his eyes multiple times and slowly turned his head toward me. He seemed completely out of it. He was a thousand miles away, but he looked at my rank and, probably out of training or respect, I could see he was thinking about responding instead of just blowing me off.

There was no interest or motivation on his part to engage in conversation; that was obvious. I wanted to respect his feelings, but I also badly wanted to know why he was apparently dissociating, so I prompted a conversation by asking him where he was from.

After a few moments of silence and uncomfortableness on my side, he finally replied, "Kentucky, sir." He looked like someone reacquainting himself with reality or emerging from a dream.

"How long have you been in Kandahar?" I asked. He shook his head back and forth this time and tried again to clear his mind. I could tell he had been in theater for a while because, compared to most people, his uniform was wrinkled, dirty, and smelled pretty bad. This is indicative of someone who often goes "outside the wire"[5] for long periods of time.

Again, it took him a few moments to respond, but he finally said, "Six months, sir."

I thought, okay, that probably means he's one-third to half finished with his tour. I asked him if that was the case.

"Negative, sir; we're heading home next week." Now this was very interesting to me. This was a typical tour of duty for an Air Force surgeon, but not an Army soldier.

---

[5] "Outside the wire" literally means going outside the perimeter of the base. The perimeter is the fence that keeps one somewhat safe from a security breach. It is often lined with Constantine wire, which is razor sharp, similar to what you see surrounding prisons in the United States.

I decided to ask the obvious. "That's kind of unusual for an Army guy, isn't it?" He again blinked his eyes several times as if still trying to clear his head. This reaction is very different than that of someone who is simply tired. This showed a lack of association with the current reality.

He actually looked me in the eye and said, "Well, sir, we're heading home after just six months." What I heard next will stay with me for the rest of my life. "You see," he said, "more than half our unit has been killed. We do maneuvers and try to find and kill Taliban, but sometimes they get us. What really sucks is that the guys who have all taken point[6] have all been killed by IEDs.[7] Now, it's my turn. And every time I take a step, I wonder if this is my last step. I wonder if I will die. I wonder if I will get my legs blown off." Then he said, "Every time I step, I ask myself, 'Is this my last step, is this my last step, is this my last step?'" He said this as if he were repeating a mantra. A tear fell from his left eye and traveled down his cheek, but he didn't seem to notice or care. It is very unusual to see a soldier cry in theater, and even more so for him not to try to hide it. He never moved a muscle. He was mentally back in the field, visualizing each and every step he had made, and would make. "But sir, I've been lucky this whole time. I don't know why God hasn't allowed me to get killed like my buddies, but he hasn't. At least not yet. I go out one more time tomorrow. I pray I don't die."

What do you say to someone at that point? What words of comfort can you possibly give? How do you answer the theological questions he posed? Why had God saved him (so far)? Did God not care about the buddies who had already died? Was he still alive simply because he wasn't on point? Why wasn't he chosen to be put on point before now? Would that have meant he would already be dead or seriously injured? What could I say about tomorrow? Good luck and that I was praying for him? I sat there with no idea of what to say. I couldn't say I'd been there. I couldn't say he would be safe. I couldn't say that God would protect him. And the truth is, I don't remember what I said, or even if I said anything at all. I may have ended up

[6] The person out in front of all the rest

[7] An IED is an Improvised Explosive Device. Our enemies often make bombs out of whatever material they have available to them that can be set off by various timers. Otherwise, if they were present when they set them off, we could immediately kill them.

with that same thousand-yard stare. I didn't want to face reality. I didn't want to think I could be talking to this kid, and tomorrow he could die. I just sat there, blinking and speechless. I think many people have struggled with what to say when they have a friend who has lost a child to death, or struggled with what to say when someone has just said they have cancer or HIV. Sometimes there are no words.

I have often thought of this young man and wondered if he made it. I wonder, even more, if he got the help he needed once he returned to the US. This was one guy that I knew for certain – even without psychological testing – had PTSD. I had come halfway around the world and seen it firsthand. As I was sitting there, still at a loss for words, a USO staffer came over and tapped me on the shoulder. "Major Tharp, we've been calling you for a computer. Do you still want to use one?"

Still in a daze, I tried to clear my head and thanked her. I didn't want to miss out on emailing my wife, but I couldn't get this kid out of my head. Truth is, I still can't. Telling this story now brings tears to my eyes, and I wonder – did he make it out alive?

CHAPTER 17: SARAH AND THE USO. DEATH OF ANOTHER US SOLDIER

There are some very cool ladies who worked for the USO, and the guys enjoyed giving them a good-natured hard time or just sitting and chatting with them because it reminded them of home. One of these guys was Daren, an Army lieutenant who volunteered with me at the USO. He was hilarious, a true comedian, and always had a smile on his face. He was always talking about his plans for the future, his family, and his now home state of Wisconsin. Wisconsin has a special place in my heart because it's very close to where I grew up, and it is where I did my internship in psychology. In fact, I later learned he was from the same town where I did my internship.

Daren graduated from West Point and was 24 years old when I met him. He'd come from a military family with his father, uncle, and brother all having been graduates of West Point. He wanted not only to serve his family, but also our country.

He was a character at the USO. He could make anyone laugh, especially the ladies. He was attractive, kind, gentle, fun loving, and also a leader. He had it all, and he did it the right way. Many times, I'd come into the USO and see a bunch of the ladies clustered around him.

The guy had charisma.

One of my all-time favorite USO ladies was Sarah. Sarah was sweet and kind and came from West Virginia. She even had all her teeth. (I'll pay for that one later!) She was always at the USO, even when she wasn't working a shift. She and the other staff often went to the DFAC just to hang out with our guys. That's how much she loved supporting our military personnel. She had a cute dimple, was petite, and a runner, so many of the single guys were interested in her, especially Daren.

The two were smitten. They were both enjoying their mutual attraction; it was rather cute and a very nice break from the realities of war. He would come in from the FOB and hang out at the USO. She would hang out at the USO and hope for an opportunity to go to the FOB. They were adventurous, fun-loving, kind, sweet-hearted people. It was so nice to see that in theater after seeing all of the crazy stuff we saw.

About once every two or three days, sometimes more often, we got an email over our secure network that went something like this: "One US soldier, KIA, Ramp Ceremony at 0340 at the flight line. Key personnel only. No sunglasses or covers (hats) allowed. Begin to form up at 0325."

Unfortunately, I had been to about ten of these ramp ceremonies in just the first two weeks I was in Kandahar. There was a time when, even though I was key personnel and allowed to go as the MEDAD, I actually stopped going. Emotionally, it was just too difficult. Your heart sinks every time you read one of those emails. One of the most emotional aspects was watching the lines form up, the casket go by as you saluted, and the faces of the 20-24 year-olds who carried the casket of their fallen soldier. It was heart wrenching. When "Amazing Grace" is played on bagpipes, and you

 watch the casket go down the flight line, and the KC-10 opens its bay doors, and the soldiers slowly walk the casket into the plane, you cannot help thinking of that soldier's family . . . and your own.

I don't know how the USO ladies did it. Honestly, they were there every time, showing respect, honoring the fallen, being supportive of those left behind. It's one thing for a psychologist, chaplain, commander, etc., to watch this. It's another when a civilian, who isn't required to be there, attends on a consistent basis. They did it because they cared.

That night, Sarah got a text pretty late from one of the other girls, informing her of a ramp ceremony and asking if she was going to go. This one was at 0300. Yes, that's 3:00 a.m. She was going to get off work at the USO (they stay open very late), close up shop, and then head to the runway. It was going to be a long night. But that's Sarah.

0335: Sarah arrived at the runway after closing the USO and saw the soldiers standing there. They were preparing to go on the runway. Remember, this is the world's busiest runway, so to stop everything requires significant command and control. After working in the Joint Defense Operations Center and seeing the intense mental requirements of the Air Traffic Controller and the Air Operations Center, I knew this was no easy feat. However, after enough practice, of which we had plenty, the system had become truly seamless. This was just a result of excellent coordination and care on behalf of our military and civilians. They are more than just America's best; they are the world's best.

Do you know the name Pete Myers? Probably not. Why do I ask? Because he's the guy who replaced Michael Jordan after he retired from the

Chicago Bulls. This guy made it to the big leagues, but he was no Michael Jordan. Same with me. The writer Sarah Kemp penned what happened in her own words. How dare I even tie her shoes? Here is her account, written days after it happened:

I had met Daren Hidalgo a time or two before when he first got in country before pushing out to his COP. I vaguely remember making a dumb joke about Hidalgo and that being the name of a

horse (thank God he didn't hold it against me). Then a few weeks later on Halloween night he and some other soldiers from his company volunteered. It was my first holiday away from home and he made me forget that I was in Afghanistan. By the end of the night I thought holidays will not be so bad with my new family out here. He was hysterical. His huge dimples reminded me of an athlete who has huge muscles because they work out so much. He had these huge dimples from smiling so much. Everyone was drawn to him like mosquitoes to a blue light, they can't quite pinpoint why, but they were captivated.

He was at KAF because he had escorted the belongings of a fallen soldier in his platoon. That night we talked about death and how no matter how much "training" he had, he was human and felt emotions about his buddy dying but he had to be strong to lead his men. That's the kind of guy Daren is, he always, without a doubt, put others first. We spent a lot of time that week just talking about everything: growing up in PA and WV (we both liked pepperoni rolls), being Catholic, choosing the military or me choosing to come out here, and especially about missing our families and friends. We debated whose mom sent better care

71

packages. He insisted his mom was "The Queen of Care Packages" because she had so much practice with him and his brothers all in the military. He said she clearly topped all other care packages because sometimes she even put in magazines with hot girls in them.

Soldiers from his unit are always coming through the center when they rotate into KAF and Shaw (one of his soldiers) told me a couple weeks ago that he had to wake Daren up and he said, "LT get up!" and that Daren immediately sat up and karate chopped his way out of his sleeping bag. Shaw said it was hysterical. I can picture it, and it makes me laugh.  Gentry, who volunteered with Daren at the center and was in his company, said, "He could always bring a smile to anyone's face and it was contagious. You couldn't help but be around him and be in a great mood."

He had sent me a message two days prior that he was going to be coming through KAF soon for some scheduled maintenance and I was excited to see him.

I got a text that night at 2324 from my coworker, "Showtime is 0340 for 1 US Army." I had no idea how that text would impact me. As a USO staff we try to have at least one person attend every ramp ceremony for a fallen soldier at KAF. I had been to about 4 or 5 previously, and since I just finished up my shift, it was my turn. I didn't see the text until 0300. It was bitterly cold that night and I was tired and honestly did not feel like going, but knew I would be honoring a fallen soldier so I got in the truck and drove to the flight line.

I was wearing a ridiculous hat with flaps on it that I felt a lil funny for wearing, so I took it off when I arrived. Soldiers from every country were chitchatting quietly before the ceremony. I spotted the general who is in charge of KAF, the one who watched me sing like an idiot to Kix Brooks a couple months before. I looked and saw the MRAP waiting on the flight line to bring forth the casket. As I looked around with my hands in my pockets fidgeting to stay warm I saw the 6 soldiers assembling to walk out to carry the casket and I stopped moving, I stopped looking, I stopped everything when I saw their unit patch: "TOUJOURS PRET" Always Ready. My heart sank into the pit of my stomach; that was Daren's unit. Although I wouldn't allow myself consciously to acknowledge that it could be him; somewhere, somehow I knew something wasn't right. This was going to be someone I knew. I walked out onto that runway and stood in line at attention across from a line of soldiers. I was concocting in my head the angry email I would send Daren. I would yell at him for not responding to my email from two days prior and making me worry that it was him. I'd ask about the deceased and hope he wasn't close with him. I'd see if he was coming soon.

The wind was whipping through the flight line. The speaker for the mic stand was swaying. I couldn't see the chaplain but I heard him speak some Bible passage that was meant to give us

 hope that the deceased is in a better place. Sometimes they say the name of the fallen soldier, and other times they don't. This time he did. The chaplain said, "First Lieutenant" and my mind sighed with relief because I had momentarily still thought Daren was a Second Lieutenant, but then I remembered he had just been promoted, "Daren" and I knew it right then and there, there are not many Darens, it was him, "Hidalgo." Honestly, I'm not even sure I heard the Hidalgo part. I

gasped aloud and saw the worried look of the soldier across from me whom I could tell was thinking, "This chick is gonna lose it." I had been to ramp ceremonies before, I usually spent my time praying for their family and friends who knew them. I would look out at the fallen soldier's unit with pity, and ache in my heart for

1LT DAREN M. HIDALGO
March 4, 1986 – February 20, 2011

their pain. Always in the back of my head I was thanking God I didn't know the deceased. My worst nightmare was imagining attending one of those for my friends. My nightmare was coming true and there was nothing I could do to stop it. I quickly told myself to get the F over it because it was happening and the ceremony would be over before I knew it and I would miss it. I would miss honoring him. I pulled it together and I stood there and I saluted him. I watched the soldiers hold him while holding their arms around each other's backs. I can still vividly see his steel casket with the flag draped over, the two female soldiers at the front, the one male soldier who looked no older than 19, the gleam off the second soldier on the right's gold wedding ring as he grasped the back of the blouse of his fellow casket carrier so fiercely his knuckles were white, the fancy writing of Mississippi on the back tail of the plane, the slow haunting music of Amazing Grace. I couldn't bring myself to turn my head and watch him be placed into the plane. I stared out into nothingness. Then it was over. We were dismissed. I thought this can't be happening, it's not real, this is a nightmare, I'll wake up. I looked back three times on my walk back across the flight line, just to make sure the plane was still there and the soldiers were still there, and this was still my life. I made it to the

74

car and immediately dialed one of my coworkers, "It was Daren" was all I could get out.

It was a shocking way to find out. But I would not want to change it. I got to stand there and honor my friend. I got to give him one of the first goodbyes. I got to stand there and honor him not just as a representative of the American public or as a USO staff or as a DOD civilian, but as his friend, someone who knew the man who just sacrificed his life. I will always be grateful for that. Being over here I don't get a chance to attend his funeral or go to a showing and see pictures and talk to his friends, all these things that bring solace in a time of grieving. I've struggled with what to write in this post. Finally, yesterday morning I woke up with the feeling that this post isn't about me, it's about sharing with whomever will listen what an amazing man I came to know. I have loved reading other posts Daren's friends have put on his Facebook. It brings a smile to my face to get to know the non-deployed Daren. In each note on Facebook, each comment on a news story online or interview on a news station, people always say the same thing about Daren, it's about what Daren did for them, what Daren did to make them happy to bring a smile to their face, because that's what Daren did. He lived for others. He died for others too. I spoke with the brave soldier who was blown up next to Daren. He said that after the explosion while Daren was lying there he was joking with him the whole time. He was telling Daren to cut it out, but Daren wouldn't stop. That's the kind of guy he was, trying to make everyone else feel better and laugh and making sure everyone else was okay, while he was the one hurting. I know that's what he'd be doing today. If somehow he could pop down here just for a lil while, he'd be telling jokes and trying to cheer us all up. The last time I saw Daren one of my favorite earrings had fallen out and he had helped me look for it, and we found the stud but not the back to it. I have since then found another back and still wear the earrings. The day after Daren was killed I worked all day and held it together. I knew he'd want me to. I did my job and helped the troops with a mostly smiling face. That night after my coworkers and I locked up, I stood at the front desk where Daren had sat and helped so many days and I lost it. I began crying. My entire day of pent up emotion came crashing out in waves of tears and sobbing.

Then I heard the tiniest sound, just a lil 'ping.' I looked down at the counter and there was my right earring, the same one I had lost and Daren found. I looked for the earring back on the floor and in my coat. It was nowhere to be found. I touched my ear again and broke out in a huge shit eating grin. I looked to the sky and said, Damnit Daren, I'm running out of backs. I shook my head and laughed, with tears streaming down my face and one earring in I whispered to him, thank you, thank you for reminding me you're still here. I'll be seeing you.

This was my first experience of trying to comfort a friend who had lost someone in the war. War had reared its horribly ugly head, and it was now up close and personal. It had taken not only someone whom I admired, but someone so young, so caring, so giving, so self-sacrificing. A true American hero.

Have you heard? Have you heard of Daren? There are over 5,000 Darens out there who have made the ultimate sacrifice in Afghanistan, and hundreds of thousands who died in our country's previous wars. Do you know any by name? Are they a family member of yours, or a friend? Are you thankful? Are you grateful? Are you? Is America? As a country, we give lip service, but what has it cost you personally? Anything? It cost Daren his life. What has it cost you?

When I returned home, a fellow psychologist and I were talking about what the future holds for our kids. She asked me point blank if I would let my kids serve in the military after what I had seen in Afghanistan. She told me she wouldn't let hers do it.

I told her that, first of all, it's not my choice, it's their choice. Secondly, how selfish was she? Honestly, it's okay for me to go and me to "allow my kids to serve" but she wanted to stay in the close quarters of the US, make money, and not ensure our way of life for the future? Are you freaking kidding me? Sadly, I'm afraid this is exactly the mentality today. Why else is the military made up of less than one percent of Americans? In the Second World War, I believe the numbers were roughly 40 percent that served, and now it is less than one percent. We are not a collective nation who sacrifices anymore. We are a splintered nation of brave individuals who sacrifice.

CHAPTER 18: INSHALLAH

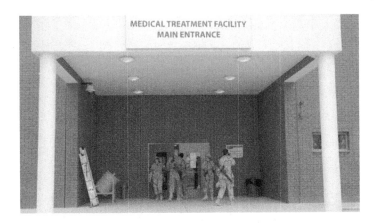

One of the bright spots in Kandahar was watching the expertise of the medical professionals and support staff at the NATO Role 3 MMU. MMU stands for Multinational Medical Unit. Affectionately known as the Role 3, it is a $60 million military medical treatment facility built in 2010 that provides medical care to Kandahar Airfield and Regional Command South. What an incredible blessing to work with such seasoned professionals. If they weren't seasoned before they came to the war, they quickly became so. Every day I saw people who had been hit with an IED, burn victims, Afghan children with various diseases, vector borne illnesses, you name it. It was amazing how many Afghan children we helped.

As we tried to "win the hearts and minds"[8] of the Afghan people, we literally had to go back to Maslow's hierarchy of needs. First, we needed to ensure that people had their physiological needs met (food, water, sleep, etc.) as well as safety and security (security of body, of employment, of

---

[8] General Petraeus preached this philosophy repeatedly. This goal of the Afghan war was drilled into our military.

resources, of morality, of the family, of health and of property). I have been trained that one of the challenges in this war (and others) is not to think like an American. With all of our biases, there are assumptions that will be made that are not necessarily going to meet the needs of the people we are trying to reach. For example, during Hurricane Katrina, we were sending tons of food via airlift. People had already moved out of the devastated area, so we had perishable items sitting in a hot and humid warehouse not helping anyone.

The Afghan homes or shelters that surround the Kandahar Airfield were often made of mud. Because of the altitude, it could get very cold. Thus, there was a need to provide for basic physiological needs. For example, they did not often have a way to heat their homes, so we met that need by providing kerosene heaters. A kerosene heater is a great source of heat and can be mobile if necessary. Unfortunately, the adults often left the responsibility of keeping these heat sources working to the children. On one occasion, one particular child was filling up the heater with kerosene and, tragically, the heater caught fire, burning the little girl over 30 percent of her body, mostly on her legs. It was not unusual to see half of the ROLE 3 trauma beds filled up with Afghan children.

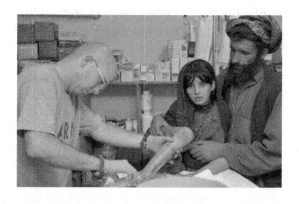

On this particular day, our medical staff was able to support this family by providing significant medical resources including pain medication, debridement[9], and burn intervention. It took several months to help this child, but because of the dedication of the nursing staff, doctors, and medical personnel, they were able to get her to a point where she could go home.

---

[9] Debridement is the process of cutting away dead skin and removing infection to the point of bleeding in order to bring about healing.

Staff members trained the Afghan parents how to take care of the child's medical needs, and there was significant joy and satisfaction when she was able to return home with her family. Personally, this situation made me feel as if we were accomplishing something good in that war-torn world. When you see so much death and destruction, it's nice to see that something good can come out of war. The staff seemed much happier than I because they were the ones who helped nurse this child back to health. Success!

It was just a few hours after she left the ROLE 3 that we received a call from our security personnel outside the base. "Security to the TOC, we have one Afghan child, GSW (gunshot wound) to the head." This was very unusual because most of the injuries sustained in Afghanistan were from IEDs. It was not uncommon to see a child who had suffered significant injuries from these horrible devices.

As it turned out, this GSW victim was the same 11-year-old girl we had spent months trying to help recuperate from the burns to her body. Our Security Forces guys were on patrol when they came across this family and discovered what had happened.

It completely devastated the medical personnel to see this child killed. During the investigation with the International Security Assistance Force (ISAF), when the father of this child was asked what happened, he responded, "INSHALLAH." God's will. I was completed confused. Had this man killed his own child in the name of Allah? As I sat there and let those words sink in, I was completely at a loss and devastated beyond any words. What do you mean, God's will? What God? What will? This was not the same God I worship. How could a father kill his own child? For those of us who actually had the courage to think for ourselves about how theology plays out in this war, this hit very much at the nerve of this war. This phrase was much like what the terrorists yelled when they flew planes into the World Trade Center, "Allahu Akbar," which in Arabic means "God is greater" or "God is [the] greatest." It was a reference to a god in whom radical Islamists believe. Their interpretation of a god whose will says that it is okay for a father to kill his own child or to fly a plane into a building in order to kill thousands of people. More importantly, it's the audacity of believing that God would want and order such an action.

As a father of two small boys, I could not even fathom this type of god. I was seminary trained for three years and for most of my life was raised in a Christian home. I learned the Ten Commandments, one of which is "thou shalt not kill." My god was a god of love, and the killing of one's own child in the name of God made no sense to me. I was completely ego-dystonic with this, meaning psychologically it did not fit my core beliefs. In fact, in my theological view, speaking for God and attributing motives to him, especially to kill, was evil. Yes, there was Just War Theory in which it is thought going to war is sometimes acceptable and necessary. That's part of the reason I was in Afghanistan. But to say and believe that God told you to kill your own daughter, that to me was evil. I still remember the intense emotions I felt when I was told by ISAF of the situation, and I cannot even imagine how the medical personnel felt after they had given countless hours of their lives in hopes this young girl could recover from her wounds. What must have been going through their minds when they learned of her senseless death?

I do not think we will win "hearts and minds" with war. In fact, I now see it as a theological war – one in which two very different theological worlds collide. The scope of this book is limited, so I will not even venture into a theological discussion about Islam and Christianity. I have no doubt that radical Islamic terrorists have made this a theological war. Although the US is both a secular and Christian nation, I can assure you there are many people in the military who think spiritually and theologically. To deny or ignore this truth is not only foolish, it's dishonest. In my world, there has already been enough deception in this war. Simply put, my heart aches horribly over the senselessness of this horrific act and the theological viewpoint and actions of the Taliban and now ISIS. The oppression of women, boys and girls, and even men in the name of Allah makes this a theological war. Do we really think this purported "surgical" approach to the war will be successful? All it has done is make surgeons of our young men and women and gotten them killed, one step at a time.

From a war standpoint, I do not have an answer. The oppressors must be stopped. Training camps where children are indoctrinated and forced to wear bombs strapped to their bodies must end. The sexual assault and abuse of girls and women must not be tolerated. The devastating blow we endured on 9/11 must be responded to with a heavy hand. To think otherwise is, in my opinion, foolish and demonstrates a blatant disregard for mankind. Edmund Burke said it right in the 1600s: evil triumphs when good men do nothing. INSHALLAH or not, this is not the God I serve. He is a God of love and justice. I will defend America with my life. That is the reason I joined the military. This young girl did nothing wrong. She did not deserve to die. When I lay my head down at night and ponder the things that happened in Kandahar, I cannot resolve them. In psychology, this is called cognitive dissonance. From a theological standpoint, I call it evil. In the Taliban view, it's called INSHALLAH. Judge me if you wish, but I hate INSHALLAH!

CHAPTER 19: THE RUSSIANS HAVE LANDED ON OUR AIRSTRIP . . . AND THEY ARE DRUNK

The Russians and Americans are not typically on the same side of a war, or at least they haven't been for the last 50 years. You can pretty much count on both of us working our military strategy through other countries to ensure that we remain relevant. The Russians were in a war in Afghanistan beginning with their invasion of that country on December 8, 1979, and continuing into 1989. When we were deciding whether to go to war in Afghanistan, their advice to us was, "Do not go." This may have been good advice. But we are Americans, not Russians, and based on our invested self-interest, we only heed our own advice.

While I was working at ROLE 3, I received a call from Flight Safety indicating there was a problem on the airstrip. When Flight Safety says there is a problem, it's significant. As I've mentioned, KAF is the world's busiest single runway. If the runway were shut down for any length of time, it could cripple our ability to prosecute the war effort. So as you can imagine, BG Kendall wanted to ensure that the runway stayed open at all times.

I wasn't expecting to hear this over my large handheld secure radio: "MEDAD, this is Flight Safety. The Russians have landed on our runway, and they are drunk. Please report to Flight Safety at Kilo Ramp." As the medical advisor, I was thinking, *What did I just hear? What am I supposed to do with that, and why are you calling me?* As was typical in Kandahar, this particular snag wasn't unusual and was left for us to solve.

I drove onto the flight line over to where the plane was sitting. It appeared that this was a stop for them on their way back to Russia. God knows it was easy enough to find; it is the world's largest cargo plane. This plane is specifically built to move a lot of freight. The only passengers are the crew. It's a wonder the thing can even get off the ground – but somehow it does. I wouldn't have liked to have been the first test pilot in this aircraft.

As I approached, I wondered how in the world I would be able to communicate with the Russians. Thankfully, they had a person on board who spoke English – broken English, but it was better than my Russian!

They had apparently decided that being drunk and landing on our runway probably wasn't the best decision either. So what do you do when you are trying to address the issue of the world's largest plane landing on the world's busiest runway when it isn't supposed to be there? Hide the pilot. Yup, they hid the pilot. Why? I'm not certain. My hunch is that by doing so, they figured that they could delay things long enough that the pilot could sober up before being scrutinized by our security guys. To complicate matters, international law dictated that we could not enter their aircraft even though they were on a NATO airstrip. So here we were playing cat and mouse. I was trying to get to the pilot while they did what they could to delay things to give their pilot a chance to sober up. To their credit, they did produce a really good imposter who clearly was not drunk . . . but not the pilot either.

I called the people at the ROLE 3 to see if we had a breathalyzer. The response: We have good news and bad news. (This, to be honest, was a typical response in a war zone.) I told them to give me the good news first. "Well, we have one," they said. "What is the bad news?" I asked. They responded: "It isn't calibrated." So, in Kandahar, we had a breathalyzer at ROLE 3, but it wasn't calibrated! Well, of course that's the case. So, without the breathalyzer as an option, I tried to figure out a solution. There we stood, Russians and Americans, on the world's busiest runway, with the world's largest cargo plane, waiting for me to assess a non-existent pilot for alcohol without any measuring device. Sure, I could do this job. Not wanting to disappoint the general (my boss), my American counterparts from Flight Safety and I all got together and came up with COAs. One of the flight safety officers was a New York City policeman. He offered to conduct a field sobriety test right there next to the runway on the pilot (once he finally came out of the aircraft). It took a little while to convince the pilot to do it, but we told him we would ground the plane until we knew he could fly it safely. I could just imagine the news stories on this one: an international incident in Kandahar with the Russians because some American psychologist playing medical advisor (without sobriety testing equipment) grounds the world's largest cargo plane on the world's busiest runway. Very catchy.

In the end, the actual pilot completed the sobriety test. I'm convinced it was the backdoor communications with NATO that actually took care of this problem. It seemed after that phone call we received from NATO headquarters, permission was granted for the Russians to fly home, despite any limitations with the pilot's capabilities. And they did, without incident. I'm guessing that particular pilot had a pretty high tolerance for alcohol given the number of bottles we saw on the plane. We couldn't have joined them even if we wanted to – it was a dry airstrip. It was just another day in Kandahar.

CHAPTER 20: MRI AND SUPREME HEADQUARTERS ALLIED POWERS EUROPE (SHAPE)

You have probably heard by now that IEDs are the signature mark of the war in Afghanistan. IEDs not only take off limbs, but also do devastating damage to internal organs, including the brain. You often end up with a coup/contra-coup, which is when the brain smacks first into one side of the skull and then bounces back and hits the opposite side, thus damaging both sides. The damage can actually be seen on a computerized topography (CT) scan.

We had all seen plenty of IED damage to the body, but there were a lot of military personnel who, when hit with an IED, believed they were fine if they did not suffer any outward physical damage. Unfortunately, this is simply often not the case. Instead, there can be axonal shearing (a tearing of the neuron), what we call mild Traumatic Brain Injury (mTBI), that can go undetected. Typically, military personnel out in the field will get hit by an IED and become dazed, confused, experience headaches, ringing in the ears, have difficulty keeping balance, memory problems, etc. This is typical of a concussion in sporting events. Time seems to be one of the best healers, but the last thing you need is to have repeated concussions or another mTBI if you have not fully recovered from the original blast. It is difficult to do neurological testing on the battlefield, so crude alternative methods are often used. Sometimes it's as simple has having the military member do pushups. If they have mTBI, physical exertion, even push-ups, can result in a significant headache. A simple test, but helpful when trying to figure out whether a person has experienced symptoms related to a concussion.

There are other "in the field" techniques to assess this type of brain injury. The Military Acute Concussion Evaluation (MACE) is often used. It is a paper-pencil test created by the Defense Veterans Brain Injury Center (DVBIC). It assesses identifying information, event and symptom history, along with the examination portion. One of the challenges we faced with the MACE was that military personnel did not want to leave the theater of war and would get ahold of the test beforehand and memorize the answers, in much the same way a quarterback will try to persuade his doctor or coaches that he is okay to go back into a game even though he has suffered a concussion. The problem is, if he has suffered an mTBI, the quarterback will often be confused and be slow to process information, throw interceptions, fumble, and be overwhelmed by the demands of the task at hand, which could cost his team the game. His brain simply cannot process information as quickly as it could prior to the concussion. The consequence of putting a person back into a war zone with this type of symptomatology is that reaction times are not as quick. And slow-reacting warriors can cost themselves or others their lives.

As you can imagine, mTBI is a very important issue for US military personnel and leadership. Call it American exceptionalism if you wish, but based on my experience in NATO, America always steps up. We stepped up when it came to paying for things in Kandahar, we stepped up when it came to funding the ROLE 3 and providing military personnel (most were

US Navy when I was present), and we stepped up when we needed data when it came to mTBI research.

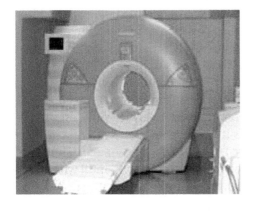

Late one night when I was in my office as the MEDAD, I received a call from a four-star general from SHAPE. I had never heard of SHAPE, and the general could tell from our conversation. He explained that SHAPE stands for Supreme Headquarters Allied Powers Europe, and it is located in Belgium. The general informed me that SHAPE had learned that the Americans wanted to put an MRI into theater. I acknowledged that I had heard something similar, and he said, "Major, you do realize that this is a NATO base, and you are a NATO asset? We here at SHAPE will support the Americans in any way we can, especially if it means getting this MRI into theater. That being said, however, we haven't been asked. And honestly, we're a bit tired of the Americans doing whatever they damn well please. So this is in your hands. You need to contact the Americans and have them ask us if they can put an MRI into theater. We, of course, will say yes, but the least they can do is ask."

I was sitting there thinking, *I don't speak for America. What am I supposed to do, call the President?*

After his speech and indirect order, I politely said, "Sir, do you mind if I ask you one question?" to which he replied in the affirmative. "I am a major as the MEDAD in Kandahar. Shouldn't this be handled at a much higher level than me?"

I could tell he was smiling even though he said, in a grumpy, coarse voice, "Yes, but we have to start somewhere, so I decided to start with you."

"Yes, general," I replied. "I'll get right on it."

WHAT? What was I supposed to do with this one? I had heard of American exceptionalism before and how the US pretty much does whatever it wants. Considering we are paying for most of it, I imagined the US felt it had the right to make most of the decisions. Oh, we all played cordially together, but when it came down to it, that was the bottom line. I was able to solve the dilemma by forwarding a request up the chain to Petraeus' office in Kabul, which sent a formal request from the US to SHAPE. Once again, I found myself shaking my head back and forth at the craziness of it all. When I prayed that I would get to do things in theater and experience everything possible, I never imagined that I would be getting a call from a general in SHAPE who could tell NATO what to do, who in turn could tell the US what to do, who in turn would tell me what to do. But then, this was Kandahar.

CHAPTER 21: AFGHAN PARTNERS

One of the benefits of going to war with coalition forces was that the burden of responsibility was shared amongst multiple nations. In this fight, we found ourselves in a completely foreign land with a different culture and an enemy that doesn't fight conventionally. This wasn't unusual for the United States. Most of our wars have been fought outside the US. In this war, we found ourselves working overtime to learn, understand, and build relationships with our Afghan counterparts in order to "win the hearts and minds of the Afghan people," according to General David Petraeus. In our weekly high-level meetings, we were "blessed" with the presence of one of the top generals who reports to the president of Afghanistan. This man happened to be a family member of a prominent official and was a general by the age of 30 because that is usually how power is arranged in Afghanistan.

We learned through trial and error that every time we shared information ahead of time about where we were going to do maneuvers or quick strikes, we found ourselves in an ambush. It didn't take long to see there was a security breach somewhere in the inner circle. So, the US decided against telling our Afghan partners where we would be going the next day. Psychologists work in correlations, and there was a 1.0 (100%) correlation between our being ambushed and telling our Afghan partners our plans. Once that practice of sharing location information was halted, the ambushes against our soldiers stopped.

Of course, with any correlation, there can be confounding variables. Although from a statistical standpoint, it didn't take a genius to figure out why every time our Afghan partners knew our plans we were ambushed, and when they didn't, we weren't.

In addition to the ambushes, we endured an Afghan pilot killing nine Air Force officers in Kabul, and numerous other incidents where Afghans killed US military members who were working alongside them. The response from HQ: "trust our Afghan partners." Let's just say that trust was a significant issue.

CHAPTER 22: CONTRACTOR DISPUTES

In a theater of war, most of what we deal with seems as if it is surreal. One cannot even fathom some of the things that happen in theater. What we do in war is not the kind of reality you want to live in for too long. Otherwise, you start generalizing your experiences to the rest of the world. For example, you start wondering if there is any place that is safe. And because we are trained repeatedly to assess and mitigate risk, it only makes sense that we would do that when we come home. It's like there is a switch that never gets turned off.

In reality, what is really important is loving my wife and my kids, taking them to school, going to work, enjoying Easter and Christmas dinners, playing sports with my kids – *that's* the real world. Seeing people get hit with IEDs and losing limbs is so surreal. Military personnel deal with more reality than we need to. We are the last ones who want to go to war. We know the impact and consequences of war firsthand.

The last thing I imagined seeing in theater were contractors getting into altercations, but this new war zone reality had many of the same problems and issues that non-war cities have.

I was sitting in my "office" in the TLS when I heard some intense scrambling and someone shouting, "I need a doctor now!" That was a very strange command given that our $60 million ROLE 3 was only three blocks away. Yet, someone clearly was in need of a physician. Most people assumed I was a physician because I was the Medical Advisor. This was exactly why I hadn't wanted to do this job. I'm a psychologist. When I explained that to the previous COMKAF, he said, "Welcome to NATO. Close enough." I thought, *No, not close enough. I haven't been to medical school.*

People are often confused about the difference between a psychologist and a psychiatrist, but clearly when someone is crying out for medical help, they probably don't really care to hear the explanation. I made some queries and used my secure radio to contact ROLE 3 to request a physician, or at least get medical personnel to where they were needed.

I overheard one of the guys who was calling for help say, "Wow, there's a lot of blood over there." I couldn't imagine what had happened, and I certainly could not have guessed. It turned out that contractors flew in and out of theater through our building at a significant rate. Military members, as I've mentioned, were not allowed to drink any alcohol in theater. Contractors, on the other hand, could drink alcohol on the civilian flights into Kandahar, but once you landed, you could not drink at KAF. One of the contractors was drinking on the plane and got angry when another contractor hit on his girlfriend. So he decided that his best course of action was to stab him.

Are you kidding me? Here we were in a theater of war where people were getting killed every day in the pursuit of national security, and I was looking at a pool of blood because someone had gotten mad and knifed a guy over jealousy. I just shook my head. Outside the wire, people were trying to kill us, and inside the wire, contractors are fighting contractors. You literally cannot make this stuff up.

DynaCorp contractor pleads guilty in Kandahar stabbing

KAISERSLAUTERN, Germany — A U.S. Army contractor pleaded guilty Tuesday to assault for stabbing another contractor with a knife at Kandahar Airfield in Afghanistan, according to a U.S. Justice Department news release.

Sean T. Brehm, 44, of Capetown, South Africa, pleaded guilty before U.S. District Judge Anthony J. Trenga to assault resulting in serious bodily injury. At sentencing, scheduled for July 8, Brehm faces up to 10 years in prison.

CHAPTER 23: ORDERS TO KANDAHAR VS. KABUL: THE DIFFERENCE BETWEEN LIFE AND DEATH

One of the benefits of having Top Secret SCI clearance and being a NATO asset in the JDOC is that we had early, detailed access to information and intelligence others did not. We often read information about how our guys were hit the night before, their location, the number killed, etc. The secure information on our network computer would read something like this: "Three US Army killed, 4 injured, IED in Kandahar Province." Sometimes there were more details, but that is classified. I don't want to go to prison, so we shall leave it at that.

One day for me was very sobering. My orders were to Kandahar in a NATO billet. The other option was Kabul, the other NATO billet. As an Air Force Officer, I had the option to choose. I wanted Kandahar because that was where a lot of the fighting was occurring, and I wasn't going to war to sit on the sidelines. I wanted the full experience. If I was going to have to leave family and live this crazy life, I darn well was going to do my part to help the war effort.

We were constantly told that we were to trust our fellow Afghans and that we needed each other; it was a symbiotic relationship that would help defeat terrorism and the Taliban. I had met a few Afghans, and they seemed nice enough. And then I read what came across our secure network: "Nine US personnel killed, Kabul, Afghanistan." How could that be? This is where high level meetings occur and where it requires not only access to the base, but identification that has been scrutinized.

How could this have happened? The more I read about it, the more intel we had, the more insight, the worse I felt deep down inside my gut. The news was a significant blow in many ways. Was it true? Could it be that an Afghan pilot actually did this? Could this be not an Afghan but an al-Qaeda operative instead? I thought there was no way that one of the Afghan pilots would have done this. I couldn't have been more wrong. It was true.

The nine US personnel were Air Force. They were working in the Joint Defense Operations Center (JDOC). They were NATO assets. They were all killed – by the very people we were here to help. I felt deflated. I felt as if I had taken a direct blow by Mike Tyson to the stomach. I was sick and angry . . . and furious . . . and then depersonalization set in. This is where you no longer even feel that you are a person. It's as if you are outside of your body, and things are not even real. How the hell could this happen? HOW?

The JDOC was supposed to be the most secure of secure places. It was inside the Forward Operating Base (FOB), inside the wire, inside a secure building behind secure doors where nobody gets in who has not been approved. Clearly, there was no safe place.

These US airmen had given their lives for this country, this war, and the Afghan people, and this was the thanks they got? Winning hearts and minds just got harder for me, General Petraeus. What made me even sicker was knowing that this could have been me, had I chosen Kabul over Kandahar.

I would have been one of those nine. It would have been my name on that list. My children would have been fatherless. Thinking about that made me angry all over again. So, when Petraeus and others said to trust our Afghan brothers, what do you think was going through my head? Probably the same thing that would go through yours. I wanted to make sure my weapon was clean and ready if called upon. I wanted it loaded –

but that was not allowed according to the UCMJ. Really? So, you mean I have to choose between UCMJ action of having a loaded weapon off safe versus possibly being unprepared in a war zone where time is of the essence? These Rules of Engagement (ROE) are not the kind one should be forced into.

These are the airmen who were killed that day:

Lt. Col. Frank D. Bryant Jr., 37, of Knoxville, TN, assigned to the 56th Operations Group at Luke AFB, AZ

Maj. Philip D. Ambar, 44, of Edmonds, WA, assistant professor of foreign languages at the US Air Force Academy in Colorado Springs, CO

Maj. Jeffrey O. Ausborn, 41, of Gadsden, AL, C-27 instructor pilot assigned to the 99th Flying Training Squadron at Randolph AFB, TX

Maj. David L. Brodeur, 34, of Auburn, MA, 11th Air Force executive officer at JB Elmendorf-Richardson, AK

Maj. Raymond G. Estelle II, 40, of New Haven, CT, assigned to Air Combat Command headquarters at JB Langley-Eustis, VA

Maj. Charles A. Ransom, 31, of Midlothian, VA, member of the 83rd Network Operations Squadron at Langley-Eustis (posthumously promoted to the rank of major on May 3)

Capt. Nathan J. Nylander, 35, of Hockley, TX, assigned to the 25th Operational Weather Squadron at Davis-Monthan AFB, AZ

MSgt. Tara R. Brown, 33, of Deltona, FL, assigned to the Air Force Office of Special Investigations at JB Andrews, MD

CHAPTER 24: SPINAL CORD ILLNESS

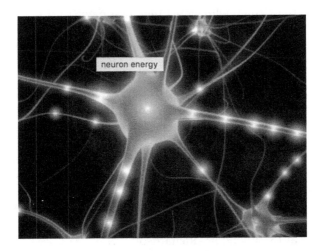

neuron energy

During my time in Kandahar, there was one phrase I used over and over: "You can't make this stuff up." This included the things that happened to people directly while they were serving in a war zone.

Six years before my deployment, I was doing a physical fitness test and felt as if I had pulled a muscle. I flew to United States Air Force Reserve Headquarters (USAFR HQ) to write part of the "Fit to Fight" program. While there, I met an incredibly talented flight surgeon. During my stay there – about three days after my PT injury – my limp got worse. Pretty soon I had to lift my leg up with my arms to get it into a car, and that triggered the flight surgeon to ask me when this all began. Turns out the man was brilliant. He asked a few questions and then said, "David, you've had a spinal cord injury."

I was totally mystified about how that could have happened. There was no injury that I could recall, and I thought if it were that serious, I would remember an injury to my spine. To make a long story short, I flew back to

Lackland Air Force Base and presented to the medical center in San Antonio, Texas, where I spent ten days in the hospital while the neurologists tried to figure out what was wrong. It seemed I was struck by a neurological demyelinating condition called transverse myelitis.

The pain in my back was so intense that I literally began crying one night. My limp increased, and I had numbness and tingling in my right leg. When I put one foot in bathwater and then the other, I discovered that I had a totally compromised temperature response. Thankfully, I was able to do extremely well in my recovery. During years four and five of my recovery, I excelled to the point where I was receiving "Excellent" scores on the physical training requirements. I was told by my neurologist that I would have a four percent chance of reoccurrence. I thought those were pretty good odds, especially because I was so active and my recovery had gone well except for some lingering issues with my right leg.

Fast forward five months into my six-month tour in Kandahar with 12-16 hour days, unimaginable stress and being triple-hatted as the MEDAD, Preventative Medicine and the Environmental Enginee. In addition to identifying military and civilian personnel who were killed in Kandahar, I also had the task of notifying the nation, military service, or contractor about their respective KIAs. I had seen enough people die to last a lifetime. I had been to so many late night (and into the early morning) ramp ceremonies for the fallen that I finally had to stop going for a short period to try to reset and balance my own mental health.

And then, for whatever reason, I had a reoccurrence of the transverse myelitis (TM). I thank God for the ROLE 3, my connections with the medical staff, and the Navy neurologist. My neurologist in Kandahar was amazing. Even without an MRI, the gold standard for treating an autoimmune disorder is with high doses of IV steroids. We began a five-day treatment with the hope that things would improve, or at least not worsen.

One of the hardest things to know is whether or not the IV steroids actually do what they are intended to do. The problem is there is no way to really test it. People do research on it and compare how others have done with and without it, but that's the best we can do. There are not a lot of people with this diagnosis and very few, if any, clinical trials. TM lesions, according to the experts, are somewhat different than the multiple sclerosis (MS) lesions. What I have since discovered is that TM is of the spinal cord only; MS has lesions in the brain. And transverse myelitis is often the first manifestation of what may turn out to be multiple sclerosis later on.

Unfortunately, I continued getting worse in theater to the point that I could barely walk. The general asked what was going on, and when I explained, he wanted to medically evacuate (medevac) me. I convinced him that back in the Continental United States (CONUS), I didn't even get treatment, and here I was already being treated. It would take days if not weeks to go from Kandahar to Kabul to Germany, then to Baltimore, then to the AF Academy, then to San Antonio Military Medical Center. However, if I could stay in place, I would continue to receive the gold standard in treatment without losing any time. The general was concerned, but the logic made sense to the point that he allowed me to stay as long as I was under the care of a neurologist. Thank God for Navy neurology. I kept my commitment to the neurologist, and the general kept his promise to let me receive immediate treatment. It was a win-win scenario, especially given that we didn't have anyone to replace me. The general didn't care about that; he cared about his troops, and it showed.

After a month in theater with this condition, I completed my tour, even going over to ensure that things were in place for the next person, and then it was time to leave. At the time, there were no direct medevac flights to Landstuhl Regional Medical Center (LRMC) in Germany. Unfortunately, we had 18 people who had been hit with an IED and needed extensive medical attention, so it was decided that a direct flight from Kandahar to Landstuhl was in order. The general made it clear that my time was up, and it was time for me to go home.

I had three hours to pack my belongings and get to the flight line. I had most of my equipment already packed, so that made it a bit easier. But it's amazing how much gear one has to carry home. I was no exception. So, I made my way to the flight line only to be told, "Thanks for getting here early. Your flight will leave in approximately 9–12 hours, so hold tight." Hold tight? Were they kidding me? Oh, right, I was in the military where "hurry up and wait" is the motto. So, I hung tight by "sleeping" on a hammock right next to the world's busiest runway and waited for my flight to Germany. Not much actual sleeping went on, but I was very happy to be leaving this place. I had missed my family terribly, and I just wanted to go home. It was time. It was my time.

CHAPTER 25: MEDEVAC FLIGHT TO GERMANY

I had finally completed my tour of duty, including the few extra days I stayed to make sure all was properly transitioned to my new best friend – at least in writing. My replacement was still in the US, so we emailed back and forth. I remembered only too well my own arrival and how my Brit friend had wanted to get out of Dodge as quickly as possible. I did not want to do the same thing to the next guy. Unfortunately, because that next guy was still in the US, there was no one to whom I could turn over my three jobs. I didn't want to leave the general without anyone, but he insisted it was time to leave.

After about 13 hours of waiting and trying to sleep in a hammock, it was my turn to board, and I was finally on the plane home. What a truly amazing, scary, and awe-inspiring experience. Here I was on a medevac flight home, the very kind of flight I had been coordinating as the medical advisor. But this one was unique. This was a direct flight from Kandahar to LRMC. Almost every other flight went from Kandahar to Bagram, Afghanistan, before heading on to Germany – a stop most people who are seriously injured do not need. Even Major General Smith, a NATO commander in charge of medical operations, recognized this, but trying to get the right planes that can take wounded out of Kandahar and directly to LRMC, no matter how logical, was not an easy logistical task. This was just another of the challenges I faced as the medical advisor in Kandahar. And yet, here I was, on the same medevac flight I had been trying to coordinate for months.

The flight is a long one – even a direct flight to Germany takes over eight hours. A C17 Globemaster does not make for a comfortable flight. Anyone who has ever been on one of these flights knows two things: they are loud, and they are cold. I remembered this from my flight into Kandahar. It was freezing, and I had even brought my sound deadening headphones, similar to ones I use when I cut down trees or mow my lawn. Usually, I have the radio on, but there isn't a radio signal at 45,000 feet, or whatever altitude we were. Even with the headphones, the sound was deafening. Stacked three high on gurneys and less than 24 inches in front of me were three of the 18 soldiers who had been hit by an IED, thus, the reason for the direct flight to LRMC. They needed the medical expertise of LRMC and needed it quickly. Loading that many injured onto one plane is a feat in itself –

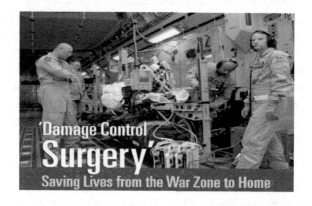

'Damage Control Surgery'
Saving Lives from the War Zone to Home

ensuring that all the medical equipment, medicine, flight doctors, flight nurses, flight commander, pilots, fuel, permissions (as you fly over other countries) are coordinated is an even more daunting task. And yet, here we all were.

I turned my attention to the wounded. One soldier who was on the top gurney was clearly in critical condition. One leg was completely gone, and his other leg was facing the opposite direction. He was on a respirator, had shrapnel wounds and bandages everywhere, and was in a medically induced coma. The monitors hooked up to this man were lit up like a Christmas tree. The flight doctors and nurses have communications between themselves, but I, of course, did not. They could hear each other talk, but because the sound was so deafening, I could not listen in. I had to go by what I could see, and I quickly realized that the doctors and nurses couldn't easily see all of the medical warning lights going off because they had so many patients to take care of. So, I found myself in a self-appointed job. I was the hand signaler when one of the lights went off. Whether it truly helped or not, I have no idea, but it at least helped me feel as if I wasn't totally useless. I would get the attention of the flight nurse or flight surgeon, point to the monitor that was going off, and they would give me a thumbs up and go to work attending to the wounded. When I sincerely prayed that God would give me every possible experience on this deployment, I had no idea what I was asking for.

My prayer was clearly being answered. Yet I was the lucky one. I decided that I would take a mental break from what was directly in front of me, walk around the plane and take a look out the small window, while thanking God I was out of the war zone. Being cooped up for eight hours on the plane was an adventure in itself. I was starving. What I didn't hear, because it was so loud, was that they had sandwiches on board for us. I saw the flight docs and nurses eating, but I wasn't about to ask them for their food. Well, what I thought was their food. To distract myself, I meandered over to some of the cargo. I stopped and stared as I read what was written on a square wooden box about 6 feet by 6 feet. "Personal effects of (and the person's name), KIA, Kandahar, Afghanistan."

Time stopped for me as I read those words. All of the cold air was nothing compared to the chilled feeling I had as I stared at those large, wooden containers. KIA – three letters I have come to really dislike. Those horrible letters represent someone's loved one – their son or daughter, mother or father, brother or sister, someone who had gone to war and was returning in a coffin. I thought about the many times I had stood on the flight line on the world's busiest runway when we would stop everything for a ramp ceremony. The same ramp ceremony where I'd stood with the men and women of the fallen comrade killed in action while "Amazing Grace" played on bagpipes via pumped in music and six soldiers carried the casket of each military member who was killed.

Each person who carried the casket was a brother in arms. I distinctly remember their faces. Their eyes staring ahead with that thousand-yard stare I had heard about and then seen and experienced with my own eyes. There were others who actually showed emotion, tearful as they carried out their duty, knowing that the man or woman who was in that casket was willing to lay their life down for them, and had.

A man closer than a brother. A friend whom they had trained with, shared meals with, slept by in the trenches, cold and hungry in an

unfamiliar land. As we held our salute and the casket was loaded into the plane, all I could do was pray for the families and loved ones back home. Just a few short hours ago, these servicemen and women were alive, fighting for our country, fighting for our way of life, fighting for the United States, fighting for freedom, but mostly fighting for their brothers who fought next to them. The same brothers who were now carrying them.

Standing in two lines, one opposite the other, it is impossible not to see the faces of those directly across from you. You notice the faces, the young faces of the men and women who are doing the real fighting. You notice their countenance and their eyes and their tears. Strong warriors who cared enough to answer our nation's call. And for what? This? You remind yourself that this is the price of war; this is the price of freedom. A grateful nation? I hope so.

But most never see this sacrifice. They don't see the pain in these young faces. They don't feel the bitterly cold night at 3:00 a.m. when this ceremony occurs. They don't see the general, who is also out there even though it means only getting three hours of sleep himself after working a 16-plus-hour day. They don't see this runway where planes of all nations and all types fly . . . and crash. They don't do an FOB walk on this same runway where we are standing for the ramp ceremony to ensure nothing flies into the jet engines that could cause it to tear the turbines apart. They don't hear "Amazing Grace" as we do. They don't pair that song with death of a comrade. The American people don't get this opportunity or heartache. So, I wonder, I just wonder, do they get it? Do they really get the sacrifice? They aren't here. We are the "less than one percenters" on the other end of the bell-shaped curve. We aren't rich; we are soldiers. We are "America's Best," and we are dead.

I then snapped back to reality. KIA. I blinked several times and tears formed, and I didn't care. I was tired of being strong. I was weary. I'd been up all night prior to this flight (because it's freaking cold and loud trying to sleep on a runway). There was not just one box of personal effects, but several. There were several boxes, all about 6 feet by 6 feet with the same label: "Personal effects of XXX, KIA, Kandahar, Afghanistan."

As my friend, Dr. A.J. Williams, says, "Heavy sigh." This is one of my heaviest sighs. I cannot get this experience out of my head, and I certainly can't convey the intensity of emotion it carries with it. There truly are no words; it is indescribable. But one thing is for sure: I am solemn, and I am respectful, and I am thankful. Thankful for those who sacrificed their lives for our freedom. This ultimate sacrifice can never be repaid. It just cannot.

And for what purpose was this sacrifice made? I felt guilty for even asking the question in my own head. Did I even have a right to ask this question, let alone say it out loud? Was there a purpose? Is there truly anything worth going to war for? Yes. I remember 9/11. That is why I joined. American freedom and sovereignty are worth it. Otherwise, I wouldn't be there. That is the big picture, but on a personal, immediate level, these men and women died while serving our country. But does our country even get it?

[ASIDE: As I write this, we are in a hotel because our house has caught fire. It could have been a total loss of the house. The boys and I were asleep while my wife Katherine, who is in medical school, was up studying, but we are safe. It's 4:00 a.m. An hour ago, my 6-year-old son Joshua called me over in a very tired voice to come and lay next to him. He reached over, pulled my hand close to his chest and cuddled my hand and quietly fell back asleep. Even today, as I edit this book six years later, tears roll down my face, and I get overwhelmed by emotion.

Is this war worth it? Is all the pain and agony from memories that are permanently a part of me worth it? It is to me. To protect my family and others, it is definitely worth it. Yes, the tears are ever present, but I am so thankful. What if I had been in Afghanistan when the fire broke out? What if it had happened three months ago when I was hit with transverse myelitis and could barely walk? What if my wife had been studying at school and not home and awake? What if our smoke alarm system hadn't worked? The "what ifs" are endless.

I ask myself, "Was this fight worth it to me?" Not just for the American people as a whole, but for my boss at work, a self-proclaimed pacifist, who sabotaged me while I was away at war. Hell, no! To be honest, it is not!

But for the touch of my son's hand and his pulling me close to feel safe and secure? Yes. It's worth every second of risking my life halfway around the world to know he can sleep peacefully at night with no fear of terrorism. So yes, it's worth it to me, for him. Because I love him, and I love my other son, Peyton, who is sleeping on a pull-out couch right next to Joshua. And for my wife who is asleep in the other room. And for my family back in Illinois. And for all those who are grateful for what we do.

But for the people who don't care, who don't show respect, for those who write horrible things on social media, or for political agendas I despise, NO! It is not. Many who serve will disagree with me on this point. They may say it was worth it to allow others the freedom to voice their opinions and speak freely. I have a more difficult time with this because I have experienced too much. Too much pain, too much heartache, too much personal loss. I'm starting to sound like my brother Joe, who experienced this and much, much more after coming home from being deployed to Vietnam.]

It had been a long eight hours when we finally landed in Germany. Our military personnel, who greatly care about us, took the most critically wounded off first. I was thankful. I could barely walk, but I had my legs. I felt so grateful to be alive. I prayed for those guys, each one of them, as they were unloaded from the plane and onto a bus to go to LRMC.

I prayed for their families, and I cried. Prayer makes me feel better. I appeal to a God I cannot see, but whom I believe in. I have changed theologically for the better. I pray that God is truly omniscient, omnipotent, and omnipresent. I want him to *see* everything, *know* everything, and judge accordingly. I want him to punish those whose hearts are evil. I want him to reward those who seek peace. I want him to give a crown of jewels in heaven to those who sacrifice and serve for the right reasons, especially those who are wounded or killed.

As I steadied my legs to deplane, I tried to keep what balance I had left. I was emotionally exhausted and overwhelmed after such a flight and finally knowing that I was out of the war zone. It was very cold in Germany at that time of year, and I wasn't wearing the heavy coat they provided us when we deployed. The three-hour notice I had to pack for my departure on medevac flights provided very little time to get my things in order. It was basically a matter of handing over my unloaded weapon before boarding (as is protocol) and then getting on the plane. The eight-hour flight was not nearly enough to decompress emotionally. Hungry, cold, and ready to get on the bus to Landstuhl Regional Medical Center, I heard, "Major Tharp, is that you?" I looked up, wondering who in the world would know me in Germany.

It was a flight nurse I went to Squadron Officer School with in Alabama! The same one who fell from the obstacle course when reaching for a wet metal bar ten feet in the air and broke her back in five places; the same woman who refused to leave despite horrible pain and who pushed through the last week in a back brace just to finish - a strong woman of courage and talent, and here she was. I couldn't believe it. I often think of her because she represents America's best, someone who would not quit or be denied. She was going to serve at all costs...and here she was. I think this goes to prove that even injured military members can still serve. Despite her disability, she persisted and was serving injured soldiers, sailors, airmen and Marines. I wasn't prepared for what I was about to hear next.

CHAPTER 26: OSAMA BIN LADEN

"MAJOR THARP, DID YOU HEAR WHAT HAPPENED?" she shouted as I hobbled down the walkway from the rear of the C17 we had flown in from Kandahar. The words sent fear ricocheting through me. As the medical advisor, I was always afraid that something like a Chinook helicopter would be shot down on my watch. I was afraid that multiple people would be seriously injured or killed at the same time, and we would suffer a mass casualty situation. Either way, I would be involved. We had recently been told of three insurgents on base, but we had no idea who or where they were. Had we been infiltrated? Was the intel accurate? Were they there?

A week prior to my departure from Kandahar, I was told by two female Army privates that three men with beards, in military uniforms but without insignias, were walking around the corner. I took off running toward them, my weapon loaded, and then the unthinkable happened: my symptoms related to the transverse myelitis put me in a tailspin. No matter what my mind wanted, my body refused.

I ran about 30 yards, and my spine literally locked up. The lesion in my spine said "enough." I couldn't move; I could only stand there. Anyone who has ever experienced it knows that the tightening around your chest that never stops feels like someone is giving you a bear hug. It never releases and is beyond uncomfortable. It makes it almost impossible to breathe, let alone move. The presumed insurgents would have to wait. I wasn't going anywhere. I literally stood there and could not move.

Now as I stood on that walkway, my mind began to race. I wondered, *Did those three ultimately wreak havoc on our base? Did a Chinook crash? Did a Chinese 107 rocket come in and hit a DFAC (again), killing multiple people? Was the general okay?* She knew something, and it had to have happened during the eight hours I'd been in the air. As fear engulfed me, I said, "Oh no, tell me what happened."

She stated, "We got him! We got the bastard. We killed Osama bin Laden."

Tears overwhelmed me. I don't know the origins of all of my intense emotions. All I know is that I couldn't hold back my feelings any longer. My head was nodding up and down, and I said, "*Yes!*" What a moment to hear this news. The timing couldn't have been better, just as I was coming out of a war zone in the heart of Kandahar. I was overwhelmed with emotion, and I stood there in tears. I felt personal joy, as if we had actually accomplished something positive. Being theologically trained, it's not in me to be thankful to God for another person's death. But I was. . . and still am. Judge me as you wish. I don't care. I'm glad he's dead. I'm glad we killed him.

War changes people, and it has certainly changed me. I will never be the same. Although I initially wondered if other military members experience this, I no longer question it. We are all changed. These are the types of experiences that change one's core beliefs. It is these experiences that cause us to have situational awareness at all times because our lives and those around us depend upon our mitigating risk. We see situations as threats, and we must ensure that we are prepared at all times. We don't mean to do it; we just do it.

We are now trained, just like Pavlov's dog, to react and respond based on stimuli. Anything new, anything unfamiliar, anything that brings about uncertainty puts us on guard. I wondered if the nine Air Force officers killed in Kabul could have done anything to prevent their deaths? Most likely not; otherwise, they would have. We all want to come home alive, so we think about this day and night. We worry and strategize and prepare to make sure all come home. And yet we know, that is an impossible task. We will not all come home.

And how does this experience affect the other 99% of the US? Does this change happen to the American people who don't witness and cannot experience it firsthand? Can they truly even understand? Not with the intensity, or to the degree, that I and others who were there experienced it.

I wonder if my brother Joe went through these emotional experiences and reactions to situations when he returned from Vietnam? I have the benefit of hindsight. I know the American people didn't witness or appreciate what he went through. Vietnam veterans received a very cold, antagonistic greeting, even to the point of being called "baby killers." So why didn't my brother write a book after Vietnam? Why didn't he get angry and fed up with all of this? He did, just in a different way. He looked to the answer of American leadership as his focus. He believes, as I do, that as the leadership goes, so goes the country.

As I write this, neither he nor I are happy with where this country is heading. Is this what we fought for? Is this what we were willing to die for? As I talk with some combat veterans, they truly have strong feelings about our government and about leadership. It is the leaders of this country, both military and civilian, that make decisions that put us into harm's way. And it's not as if we don't know there is invested interest. There is. Money rules, and so does oil and corruption and more things than I can even imagine that truly happen, even without my knowledge.

The backdoor deals, the deception, the greed. And it's one of our own that dies. We tell ourselves that it is not in vain, that it is for an ideal world we believe in. And yet, we know that this is not always the case. And we get angry because we know firsthand the sting of war. We are resentful but fear what will happen if we speak out. As a matter of fact, you cannot have an opinion or voice about these things when you are in the military. You can be court martialed for expressing those opinions. We are soldiers, and it is our job to serve without question. And we do. But there comes a time when we are no longer bound, either legally or by our own fear.

I truly believe most people are not willing to make the sacrifice it requires to be a part of the military. They want their freedom. They want their money. They want their time. They want their rights to say and do as they please. They want. This is the opposite of sacrifice, selflessness, and service. It is the opposite of what John F. Kennedy famously said: "Ask not what your country can do for you, but what you can do for your country," It is American pride at its worst, and it comes at the expense of that less than one percent. What a blessing to sit at home and "support our troops" and yet be able to say, "I'm not going to let my son or daughter join the military," which is exactly what was said to me by one of my coworkers upon my return to work in the States.

Um, so I'm willing to die, but you aren't. In reality, I don't want someone like that serving next to me. You don't have what it takes. Just stay home in your comfortable house, in your comfortable bed, sleeping peacefully at night knowing someone *else* is ensuring your freedoms.

It is no wonder that anger can get the best of us when we have these experiences. Yes, we are changed, no doubt about it. But you would be changed as well if you were in our boots. We are all the same, just a product of our choices and experiences. We need to be in this fight together. We need each other.

CHAPTER 27: WE ARE FINALLY SAFE NOW THAT WE ARE OUT OF THE WAR ZONE AND CAN LET OUR GUARD DOWN - WRONG

Now that I had finally made it out of Kandahar alive, I was literally overwhelmed with emotion. The first time I saw grass, I laid face down on it, smelled it, ran my fingers over and through it, feeling every blade, and in that prone position, I cried.

But when you haven't seen any color (except at the USO) for nine long months, the bright green color of grass and its earthy fresh smell can be joyfully overwhelming. It reminds you of things that are fresh and alive. The opposite of death, dying and destruction. Thank God for Landstuhl Regional Medical Center (LRMC) in Germany.

At LRMC, it was healing time. One of the very best things about being in war is how much you appreciate everything when you are *out* of a war zone. The two weeks I spent in Germany at one of the best hospitals in the world were truly amazing.

From the moment we stepped off the plane and onto the bus that would take us to LRMC, it was a truly awe-inspiring experience. Someone clearly integrated Lean Six Sigma principles! I have never seen anything so organized and choreographed.

There were two people serving as concierges for each injured military member on our plane.

The first thing they did was put an orange vest on each soldier to indicate they were coming out of a war zone and had been injured. Each soldier was assessed based on the severity of his or her injuries and taken care of accordingly. To say they took good care of us would be a gross understatement. Most people have heard of the Walter Reed debacle. This was highlighted in the *Washington Post* coverage of the deplorable conditions that our service men and women were experiencing at the largest Army hospital in the United States. This has now been resolved. LRMC was the exact

opposite. This was high-level care at a state-of-the-art facility with people who genuinely cared. Most are military, and there is a palpable (and welcome) sense of pride and appreciation.

I had my checklist and every test, every assessment, was on that checklist. They went over it and checked every possible thing I could possibly need. I needed an MRI, so my concierges took my chart directly to the MRI lab, and I was told, "Go get chow and come back in 2 hours. We will be ready for your MRI." I couldn't believe it. That would take 2-3 months in the US. They cared about the warfighter first, at all costs, even to the point of realizing we may not have eaten on the flight and providing us with food. They walked us (yes, walked us) to where we needed to go. They held our hands. They pushed our wheelchairs. They loaded the gurneys, *and they cared.* **These were God's angels.**

This was the kind of response I now expected from myself as a mental health provider and how I would treat my future patients when I returned to the States. After all I'd been through, I was changed forever. What would be difficult was figuring out how to help my peers and service family members *get* it. But how do you package a lifetime of experiences from a deployment into a tangible product that people will "get"? I had no idea, but I was going to try.

The chaplain's closet was a place where one could pick out civilian clothing because all you had with you was military clothes. The chaplains were amazing. I am so appreciative that I can't even find the appropriate and specific words I want to express my gratitude. When you come out of a war zone, it's certainly not a vacation. The only clothes you have are those on your back. The chaplains have a closet (more like a huge room) where they have donated clothes that you can wear. Hey, wearing civilian clothes after being in a military uniform for the past year is a treat. What? No boots? We can wear shoes again? And jeans, are you kidding me? It's like coming back to a whole different world. Even this experience changes you.

The chaplains help you transition back into the "real" world. It's hard coming back to that world, as much as you've looked forward to being there.

In fact, Navy Captain Michael McCartney, in the picture on the right, who had been the ROLE 3 commander for almost a year when I left, said that he sends his doctors and nurses home after four months. Most of them want to stay, but he won't let them. He understands people want to make a difference and help our war fighters. It's honorable and very worthy  work and much needed. These people are the reason, along with the medevac folks, the medics, and the combined medical incident response team, that we had a 98 percent viability rate in Kandahar. If people made it to ROLE 3, they had a 98 percent chance of survival. The highest in any theater of war. But even so, or perhaps for that very reason, Captain McCartney refused to let them stay after four months. His philosophy is "This isn't real; this is a war. Go home to your family. Get out of here; you've done your job. Now it's time to get back to reality."

I didn't understand or appreciate his wisdom until I got out of the war zone. You get caught up in it. It's addictive. You don't want to leave because you have people that count on you. Their lives are on the line, and you know they wouldn't just leave you. So, it's hard to leave, especially once you've figured out your role and learned how to be effective and efficient (Two traits I have since learned you do not always encounter in the States.) But in a war zone, people's lives are on the line. You have to do it right; otherwise, people die. And sometimes they die anyway, despite your best efforts. It was my job to coordinate medical response at KAF, identify the people who died, and coordinate their body back home. People die in war; that's the reality. You get used to it, but really, you don't.

After a few days of multiple tests, they gave us some down time. The chaplains had a sign-up sheet for people who wanted to get away for a few hours and check out Germany. This ministry is truly a godsend. Trying to transition back to normalcy is hard enough. Besides being overwhelmed from being injured and getting to see grass for the first time in months, you suddenly realize you haven't heard a happy, singing bird in almost a year. When you first hear one, you realize the transition back to the civilian world is going to take a while. The chaplains know this. They don't preach to you. They take you alongside them, and they show you the beauty of the land and the people of Germany. Just think about how 75 years ago, we were trying to destroy this land, and its corrupt government. Nowadays, our enemy is the Taliban and ISIS. See how quickly you slip back into war thinking? It was time to shake it off and slip into a new reality.

I had only seen pictures of castles in books. To see them in person was awe inspiring. The history is amazing. You realize just how miniscule you are in this world when you look at how old some of these castles are. And these are the ones that survived the Second World War. The country is

beautiful. It would be like destroying a rundown American city, razing it, and starting over, only with a gorgeous, picturesque landscape for miles and miles

and miles. The Rhine River is stunning as it weaves through the country. I could live there. It's that beautiful. The chaplains made this all happen.

They escorted us around the country and they fed us – this is the cup of cold water they gave us, and we drank it up. We were so thirsty, so needy, so exhausted mentally and physically and spiritually. Jesus had it right . . . a cup of cold water is exactly what a dry, thirsty person needs. God bless the chaplains' ministry in Germany.

After my two weeks in Germany, getting MRI tests, blood drawn and various assessments, it was time to head to the US. This is when being a reservist is a challenge. The Air Force takes care of its active duty counterparts, but when it comes to reservists, not so much. It was impossible to find anyone that could help me, and when I did, they were like, "Oh, we don't know what to do with a reservist." Gee, thanks for my service! It was very frustrating. I realized when they didn't understand the importance of a Line of Duty (LOD), they didn't get it. For a reservist, you have to have documentation that you were injured in theater; otherwise, it's undocumented, and if it's undocumented, it didn't happen. At least my training taught me how important that documentation is to the VA. Unfortunately, they didn't even know what an LOD was! UGH! My trek back to red tape had begun. I really didn't want or need that hassle. Trying to walk was hard enough.

When we finally got on the bus and were ready to leave, we were told to make sure that we wore the clothes we got from the chaplains' closet, or the clothes we had bought with the money they gave us. It was actually weird having money, because I hadn't used it in quite some time. In a theater of war, you don't use money. Well, at least until you try to buy food from the boardwalk or items to take home with you. Dealing with the local Afghans is a complicated story in itself. Oh, by the way, I've forgotten to mention that the only time we never got hit with a rocket was on Saturday mornings when the local Afghans came to sell us their wares. Total coincidence, I'm sure. It seems that trying to make sense of the war is like this chapter. Things jump in and out of your thought process all while you are trying to make sense of everything that has happened.

It isn't until you finally get off the bus to catch a plane home that you start to let your guard down. It takes time. You've been trained to respond to rocket alarms and rocket attacks. Each time you hit the ground, wait two minutes, and then head to a bunker. No rockets go off in Germany, but you're hyper-everything: hypervigilant, hyper-aroused, all of your senses have been elevated and trained for war. It is classical conditioning at its best. But war is not reality . . . this is. Or, so you tell yourself. Trying to convince your body is a whole different story.

While I was in the German airport, in my civilian clothes and my military backpack, I was approached by an armed US Air Force person. "Are you in the military?" she asked. I looked at her, then I looked at her uniform and weapon and thought, I'd better say yes. "Come with me," she said and started walking. "And don't speak," she added. So, I followed her into a large room, and she asked my name and rank. I still had no idea what was going on, so I asked for some identification from her. She presented her ID and said, "Two months ago, a person came into this airport and killed three US airmen. We don't want that to repeat. I could tell you are US by your bag; you even have your name on it. I suggest you take that tag off and stay in this location."

So much for my fantasy that military life and civilian life of safety were separate. I wasn't as safe as I thought. I began to wonder when I could let my guard down. When were people going to stop trying to kill me?

As a psychologist, I have a much deeper understanding of why military members are hypervigilant and hyper-aroused. It's what's kept us alive!

You'll recall that had my orders been to Kabul instead of Kandahar, I would be dead. Every one of the US Air Force military personnel that was in the JDOC in Kabul was killed while I was in the JDOC in Kandahar. When am I supposed to stop having reactions to certain noises, alarms, smells, etc.? Go to war for almost a year, have people trying to kill you, shoot rockets at you, poison your food and water, see people get killed, witness a friend die, and then you tell me.

You begin to wonder, "Am I normal? Is there something wrong with me?" This is exactly the question I started with when I began to write down what I had been feeling when it came to war. I didn't start out to write a book on how to treat Post-Traumatic Stress (Disorder) but after about a year of writing and putting my thoughts down on paper, I realized that what was being taught for PTSD treatment and my experiences were very, very different. There was a significant disconnect between the two. As I researched it, I began to understand why. Most people who write the curriculum for PTSD treatment do not have PTSD. They are researchers. They write what people tell them. But this requires the researcher to know what to even ask. Sometimes they hit the mark, sometimes they don't. But what is certain is that they do not feel the intense emotions and overwhelming feelings that we feel. This was experiential for us, not an academic goal to publish findings and make a name for ourselves. We are about service and sacrifice. This war costs us friends and battle buddies. It is personal.

Some researchers are sensitive to this, but honestly, many are not. When you get $4 million to study a particular treatment and that treatment is at its core basis drawn from female sexual assault, you certainly don't want the data to show it is ineffective. Otherwise, what other answer is there? Sometimes any answer is better than no answer. And honestly, that is the problem with our current treatments. We've taken answers from female sexual assault victims and superimposed them onto combat veterans. They are *not* the same!

I ended up putting all of my thoughts and feelings into a new treatment for combat veterans based on the combat veteran perspective, not from a theory. I personally had had enough. It was time to do something different. And that is how the Combat PTS(D) Reintegration Program was created. It's part of our Resiliency Formation Therapy series. It wasn't created by brilliant design; it was created out of pain and an attempt to find answers in the midst of chaos. It was created to offer solutions that actually made sense to me as a psychologist. It was not something created by someone who hadn't been to war.

Cognitive Processing Therapy and Prolonged Exposure (both evidenced-based treatments for trauma) were created by females studying PTSD in female sexual assault survivors. They are good treatments for that specific population, but it is a mistake to superimpose them onto combat veterans. As I was dealing with these feelings and thoughts, I had to come up with solutions that worked for me. In the end, the feedback to our PTS(D) workbook is that combat veterans can relate. We've been there, and we've experienced the carnage of war. I do not believe that PTS(D) has to be permanent. It can be addressed, and there is hope. I've not only witnessed it but experienced it. There are answers.

POST-DEPLOYMENT

CHAPTER 28: DIAGNOSIS PTSD – ARE YOU KIDDING ME? I'M A FREAKING PSYCHOLOGIST

PTSD is a serious condition that should NOT be taken lightly. PTSD, although only formally defined and introduced into the Diagnostic and Statistical Manual in 1980, has been around since war started. In the Bible, we see themes of mental distress in the Book of Job when he is plagued by the death of his family, boils all over his body, and having his home and animals destroyed. I would argue that PTSD goes even farther back to the experience of trauma and loss when Cain killed Abel. I can only imagine what Adam and Eve experienced after one son killed the other.

According to psychologist Edward Tick,[10] PTSD has had over 80 names associated with the symptoms. Some of these are Nostalgia, Homesickness, Soldier's Heart, Hysteria, Railway Spine, Shell Shock, Battle Fatigue, Combat Exhaustion, Stress Response Syndrome, and so on.

---

[10] http://io9.gizmodo.com/5898560/from-irritable-heart-to-shellshock-how-post-traumatic-stress-became-a-disease

Veterans experience common themes from a war zone: fear of being killed, seeing people die, experiencing firsthand being shot, hit with shrapnel, reexperiencing memories related to the trauma and not remembering events that happened, among other things. These are often called the "invisible wounds of war."

The last person one should diagnose is oneself. So, I'm not making an argument one way or the other in regard to whether I should, or should not be, diagnosed with PTSD. I will, however, tell you the process by which this assessment occurred.

You Can't Make This Stuff Up.

After I suffered my spinal cord illness and stayed another month in theater to complete my job, it was finally time for me to go home. Unfortunately, because 18 of our brave soldiers were hit by an IED and RPG attack, there was a very unusual medevac flight that was then scheduled to leave from Kandahar and fly directly to LRMC. I was on that flight as I talked about earlier. It was extremely emotional and sad for me to ride out of Kandahar with these young men in such terrible shape. That ride out of Afghanistan seriously impacted me, but not in the way you might think.

At LRMC you go through a lot of assessments. I believe this is a good thing, especially given all that our men and women experience during a deployment. War is hell on many fronts – not just for those on the front lines. I'd had my share of "war" as well. Even though the general I worked for was awesome, the nature of my job was crazy. God was good to me, and I made it out alive, but not unscathed. Now it was time for me to move on, or so I thought. Yeah, not so fast.

While at LRMC, one of the assessments you receive is for brain injury, as well as PTSD. During my own assessment, as a psychologist who studies PTSD, I found most of the questions unsurprising. I still answered them honestly. As the civilian provider asked me questions, I thought back about my experiences. I felt thankful just to have made it out alive, especially given the massive loss of life I had witnessed, along with the pain and suffering I had not only experienced firsthand, but had seen others go through. Those 18 guys on the flight to Germany were enough for me, but the truth was, I had seen well over 100 people who had been seriously injured or killed. Honestly, it was probably more but I didn't want to count.

Before diving into the assessment, let me just say that I truly believe I am normal. Very normal. To a fault. I am also resilient. As I write this, our 4800-square-foot house has just been nearly destroyed by a fire. We could have lost our lives, and I am keenly aware of mortality. I've performed probably 20 funerals as a minister, worked for a Level 1 trauma center back in the States, just been through war, and now this personal disaster. I like P90X's motto: Bring it. I truly believe I'm pretty resilient, mostly based on necessity and training. I also believe I have been inoculated to things like PTSD pretty darn well.

I have all the education necessary to combat PTSD. When I was deployed, I had already been a psychologist for 12 years. I've now worked as a psychologist for the Department of Justice, and my training and work at the Level 1 trauma center in Champaign, Illinois, helped train me well. Being a Boy Scout, being prepared was ingrained in me, and I have a strong spiritual background and personal relationship with God. If you added up all my strengths and compare them to my weaknesses, I would most likely end up on the positive side of the bell-shaped curve. Overall, I would say I was pretty normal and inoculated.

But I went to war, and all hell broke loose. No kidding. From the minute I landed until the minute I left, my refrain was, "You can't make this stuff up." From corruption (both internal and external), to working as a NATO medical director and dealing with 28 countries, to learning (or trying to learn) new languages, to seeing death firsthand, to working with Afghans who would be on our side one minute and then fire a rocket at us the next, to water poisoning mitigation, to losing our computers to a "security risk," to millions of US dollars in briefcases, to watching 18-year-old "kids" serve valiantly, to rocket attacks every day (and night) . . . well, you get the picture.

It was finally time for me to be assessed. As a psychologist, a psychological assessment is a bit like a physician having to go through a proctology exam. Even worse because I know what's in my head. So, the social worker began the interview.

Q: Were you in a war zone?

A: Yes. I just came from Afghanistan.

Q: Did you see anyone get killed?

A: Uh, yeah.

Q: Did you experience any rocket attacks, IEDs, or explosions?

A: Did I mention I was in Kandahar, Afghanistan? We got rocketed every day. So, yes.

Q: Were you afraid for your life?

A: Are you serious? I just told you we . . . okay, yes.

Q: Did you witness or experience anyone die or see any mutilated bodies?

At that point, I just looked at her. More like stared at her.

A: Okay, um, ma'am, let me try to explain this. I was the medical advisor, and my job was to identify anyone who got killed in theater.

That is when she said, "Well, you don't have to get snippy with me."

The whole point of my going to Afghanistan was to better understand what people go through so I could be the most helpful provider possible. In front of me was a person asking questions and being completely clueless about the impact these questions were having on me. How did she not have situational awareness? Oh, wait. That's a military thing. I began to sense some anger building up inside me.

Q: Did you have any problems sleeping?

It was at that point that I concluded she had no idea what it is like to go to war. Otherwise, she would definitely not be asking me insane questions like these, or at least she could have prefaced it by saying she had to ask certain questions, although she could probably decipher the answer fairly easily and been more kind, compassionate and sensitive. The questions were equivalent to asking a chef if he knew what an egg was. My patience was running a little thin after everything I had been through. I just wanted to go home, my body was in pain, I could barely walk, and I was exhausted. During the interview, all I was getting were these really stupid questions when you think about the context. Of course, I had sleeping problems. We were awakened every night by rocket attacks or by our response to those attacks with 50 cals and Howitzers that created a lot of loud havoc. I decided I'd better just answer her questions and not try to enlighten her. Anyway, I was tired, and I just wanted to get this over with.

A: Yes, I had problems sleeping.

Q: Did you lose or gain weight?

A: Yes. I've probably lost 15 lbs.

Q: Did anyone you know get killed?

(A good friend of mine had died in theater, but I didn't want to think about that – I just wanted to go home.)

A: Yes.

At this point my observing ego[11] had kicked in, and I was thinking that none of this sounded good. I was getting frustrated because I felt as if the person interviewing me had no clue about what people who've been to war go through, even though that should have been a prerequisite for the job.

Q: Did you experience any loss of reality?

A: No.

Q: Did you experience any emotional numbing?

---

[11] The observing ego is like a camera looking down at you. You have the ability to watch yourself, your reactions and see how things are going.

(I knew exactly what she was asking. She was asking whether I had time to process in theater, and the answer was no. There wasn't time. I had a mission to do.)

A: Yes.

Q: Did you experience any time that you cannot recall certain events?

(I was so done with these stupid questions. My patience was almost gone.)

A: Of course.

Q: Do you feel as if your life is different now compared to when you first got into theater?

(Was she freaking kidding me? How could it not be? This was ridiculous.)

A: Yes!

That's when she said, "Well, I think you have an anger problem underlying all of this. Have you considered anger management classes?" All I could think was that if I choke her it will not look good for my military career, and promotion would be out. I regained my composure, calmed myself down and just answered the questions as if I were on autopilot. I had resigned myself to the fact that she was not going to get this, and I did not have the time or energy to help. Nor did she even seem interested.

Q: Did you experience any head injury?

A: No.

Q: Do you view the world differently?

A: Yes. (Can I go home now?)

And on and on it went....

Finally, at the end of all of the questions, she said, "Well, Major Tharp, I'm concerned you may have PTSD, anger problems, and depression. I think we need to have you further assessed."

At that point, I realized that not only had I changed, but I was very intolerant of people who have no idea what they are doing and are insensitive to the experiences of people who go to war. I know it wasn't her fault; it's a series of questions that have to be answered, but I was the patient, and I didn't have the patience or energy to educate her. I just wanted to go home. I sat there, sighed, and wondered if this is what military members go through with providers who want to give them a questionnaire, assess how they are doing, and not really understand why a person would get impatient with them?

It wasn't the veteran's issue, it was the provider's!

Right then I decided I would never treat a veteran in this manner. Even if a diagnosis was warranted, I would explain my reasoning and help them to see how it is their experiences that have led them in a certain direction.

What I would not do is simply illustrate to them that there was something wrong with them, diagnose them, and then blame them for feeling the way they did. Yes, I was changed forever; there was no doubt about that.

CHAPTER 29: THE MILITARY HOSPITAL EXPERIENCE

Just when I thought I had experienced everything the Air Force could do to me, I learned that I was wrong. Welcome to one of our nation's military hospitals. To say I was stressed from all of this decision making about my future, including having to go back to an intense working environment at the VA, would be an understatement.

In fact, no fewer than three neurologists have indicated to me that stress is a substantial trigger of reoccurrence of symptoms related to my condition. Consequently, I do everything I can to ensure that I do not get stressed out. You'd think that would be pretty easy for a psychologist. It's not. The night before I was to go before the Medical Evaluation Board (MEB) (in order to be assessed as to whether or not I was still fit for duty after my spinal cord issue), I was nervous, but excited. I was told that I could have submitted my paperwork as my lawyer had suggested, but I wasn't interested in being "disabled." I wanted to serve.

At 0500 the morning of my MEB, I awakened to an excruciating pain in my back. When I tried to lean forward and get out of bed, I felt a lightning bolt shoot through my spinal cord. *No, this cannot be happening,* I thought to myself. I laid there for a few minutes, thinking maybe I had torqued my back and that was the problem. So of course, I tried it again. I got the exact same response with the electricity bolting all the way to my toes. No way can this be happening. God, I asked for a sign. Please tell me this isn't it. It was exactly what I thought it was. Stress was causing my symptoms to flare up again.

There were two times I had these symptoms. The first was in 2005/2006 when I was in the Lackland AFB hospital for 10 days, trying to figure out what was causing my symptoms. The second time was in Kandahar, Afghanistan, in 2011. I had gone six years without symptoms until it happened in Kandahar, and now it had only been a year and a half between flare-ups.

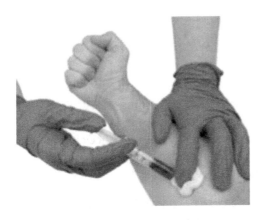

During the first occurrence, I received IV steroids and recovered to near full functioning in a short time period. The second time, I was treated in theater within a week of onset with high doses of steroids again. So, I knew I would have to make a decision: act as if nothing were happening and basically try to fake good health, or get the steroids quickly to see if I could minimize any impact and hopefully not lose the use of my legs (as I had done previously).

I decided it was best to be honest and seek medical attention immediately. I went to the emergency department at the military hospital and was stuck 14 times with a needle to get blood. (Yes, 14 times – let's just say that it is a teaching hospital.)

Then I was admitted to the hospital under a medical team with a consult to neurology. I had an MRI. Then I was evaluated by a neurology resident and her supervising staff neurologist. After evaluation, the staff neurologist said, "Major Tharp, I think we've figured out what might be wrong and why you are having all these symptoms." At last, a professional who could make sense of all this. He was a neurologist who had seen the MRI results and who knew what this was. He was someone who could finally shed light onto this disorder.

"Okay," I said. "I'm so glad to hear that. Please tell me, what is it that I'm dealing with?" I was afraid, but also encouraged by the prospect of finally having an answer.

He looked me in the eye and said, "I don't know if you are ready for this." Then I became nervous about what in the world I might have. I knew how painful what I was experiencing was. I knew there was an electrical shock which went down my spine when I leaned my head forward. I knew I was scared, but I wanted to know what it could be.

I said, "I'm ready, sir, just tell me what I'm dealing with. I need to know."

"I don't think you are ready to hear this," he said a second time. By then, I was thinking, *Just tell me what it is.*

What I said was, "Doc, I really need to know what is going on."

He then indicated to me that he felt I was malingering (faking it).

What? I was in complete and utter shock.

"Excuse me?" I said. "What did you say?"

He repeated himself. I looked around to see if I was on camera. I was blown away. Clearly, this man did not know me or anything about me. I was the guy who had just been with the Secretary of Defense, Secretary of the Air Force and the Air Force Association for winning the Air Force Association Department of Veterans Affairs Employee of the Year award. I was also the number one rated Biomedical Services Core (BSC) officer in the country. I had also won the third highest DOD award for a NATO deployment for a US military member. I had written a book and was a clinical psychologist.

I was on the cover of *Air Force Magazine*. And to top off everything else, *I had spent the last year and a half physically training to ensure I could stay in the*

Air Force. This wasn't a pride issue. I was honestly blown away that anyone would draw his conclusion based on my symptoms and my history.

I decided to see what would happen. "Really?" I said. "I find that interesting." That is when he recommended that I go back to billeting and head home. When I told my wife, she stood there and just stared at me. After a few moments of us standing there, she finally broke her stunned silence and asked, "Are you kidding me right now?"

"No, honey, I'm not."

The next morning, I received a call from the case manager for the MEB to see how I was doing. I realized that night that things were getting worse in my hands as I was no longer able to type. I was a guy who had been able to type 70 words a minute since high school, and now I couldn't even use my hands. So, I told her the truth. I couldn't feel my hands, and things had gotten worse. This was not what she wanted to hear and asked, "Then why did they release you?"

At that moment, I shook my head and spoke into the phone. "Because they think I'm faking it," I replied. There was total silence on the other end of the line. I realized at that point that she, too, was in a quandary.

She thought for a minute, then said, "I think you need to come back to the hospital."

I said, "Unless the neurologists say I have to, I'm not coming back." Even I can only handle so much. I had been through enough, and I truly no longer wanted anything to do with military medicine. At that point, she asked permission to call neurology and, reluctantly, upon encouragement from my wife, I acquiesced, and permission was granted.

She called me back about ten minutes later and said the neurology department would like me to go back through the emergency department, and they would see me there. I agreed to go, thinking somehow this could finally be fixed.

Fourteen hours later (yes, 14 hours later), in the emergency department, I was seen by the same resident who was working with the attending neurologist prior to my discharge. I suspect that the 14-hour wait to be seen was likely largely punitive given my previous experience with them the day before. This resident neurologist was superficially nice, but it was clear she already had her mind made up that I was malingering. She listened to my symptom picture, told me about not finding anything on the MRI results, and then said she had drawn her own conclusion. At this point, I was interested in hearing what she had to say. So, I asked, and she answered with confirmation that they still felt that my symptoms were intentional and that I was malingering. To this day, I am baffled. I was doing everything I could do to stay in the Air Force, not medically retire.

This was getting ridiculous. My symptoms were now causing weakness and poor fine motor coordination in my hands, and they thought I was faking! I shook my head. She said that she and the attending had discussed it, and they thought it best to get a psychiatric consult for me. I sat there dumbfounded. I knew the symptoms were the result of a real neurological problem, but how could I prove it? I am a psychologist, and they wanted a psych consult! I was on a blood pressure (BP) monitor, and my BP went to 180/110. That, my friends, is not a good thing.

I had refused any more IVs as they had stuck me so many times, and the policy was that a patient couldn't be admitted without an IV. I refused. Stalemate. The psychiatrist made her way to my room and introduced herself. She probably was about 26 years old. How in the world could she have already made it through medical school?

She looked at me, introduced herself, looked at my BP monitor, and said, "Well, that's a little high." My "anger" was clearly getting the best of me at that point. I had had enough! I said something to the effect of: "Look, Doc, you are a psychiatrist, and they've sent you to do a psych consult. I'm a psychologist. We are in the ED. You want to do your assessment and get home. I just want to go home. So, I'm sure you've heard by now the neurologists think I'm faking it. Well, I'm not, but you cannot know that. Plus, you aren't going to be doing therapy with me because, well, you're a psychiatrist. You prescribe meds. So, go ahead, prescribe me an SSRI or an SNRI, and let's get this over with."

She was a little baffled at that point. "Do you think you need it?"

Fair enough. "No, but it will get you out of here, and you can write your notes. Fact is, the anti-depressant you give me won't take effect for another few weeks anyway. So why don't you just write the script, document you saw me, and we can be done with this."

In retrospect, I felt badly about the way I treated her and this whole situation, but I hadn't asked for this. Instead of being given support, I was given the opposite treatment. Had the neurologists done their job, listened to me and done a better neurological exam, we would have never gotten to this point. Instead, they relied solely on their imaging equipment. Because there was no lesion on the MRI (yet!), they believed my symptoms could not possibly be the result of a neurological problem. Wasn't being attentive to the needs of our warriors part of the exact reason I wanted to deploy in the first place? I wanted to understand firsthand what my patients' experiences were like. *I was getting a firsthand experience of what not to do!*

Ultimately, they decided it was best to admit me, and I didn't want to go against medical advice (AMA). So, I complied. The next morning, the husband of the female neurology resident, who also happened to be a neurologist, came in to assess me. All I could think was that there was no way he was going to disagree with the attending and his wife, so this was a lost cause. I sat there defeated. I'd been through a war, been to hell and back, seen more death than I wanted to think about, was exhausted, angry, frustrated, confused and experiencing severe numbness and tingling from my chest down. Yet, I thought, I'm psychologically stable and no matter what, I'm resilient. I would not be defeated.

After an actual assessment, the doc looked at me and said, "We have a problem."

"Yeah, no kidding." I said. I was thinking in my head that we have a problem in the Air Force with neurologists, but I didn't want to say what I was really thinking.

He said, "No, seriously, there is a problem."

My sarcasm finally began to diminish. I asked, "And what is that, Doc?"

"You don't have any reflexes."

Fortunately, or unfortunately, thoughts come very quickly, and my frontal lobe had had enough inhibition.

I said, "Well, there's a reason for that, Doc. I can fake a non-reflex."

He looked at me dumbfounded, and after about 30 seconds of staring at me said, "No, you can't."

"Yes, I can. I'm that damn good. I'm so damn good that I can fake a non-reflex."

He looked bewildered. About two minutes went by before he looked directly into my eyes and said nicely, and very slowly, "You cannot fake reflexes."

I said, "I know, and so do you. You know the truth. I'm not faking this. And you also know our core values in the Air Force, so the real question is what are you going to do?"

I assumed he was a resident, and because my wife was going through med school, I knew that residents typically do not openly disagree with their attending. My wife later told me that he was not a resident, he was an attending and that is probably why he was willing to respond the way he did.

I said, "Just ask me if I am in pain." He wondered why I would ask that. I told him, "I'm leaving this hospital today, with or without your approval, but I'd rather not have to go AMA. Either way, I'm leaving. So, please ask me the questions you need to get me out of here." And, that is how I left the military medical center. Well, sort of. It was actually after I received a bill for $28,000!

Three days later at my home in Waco, Texas, I was in so much pain I couldn't stand it. I was awakened by excruciating pain in my back. I awakened my wife at 4:30 a.m. On the way to the hospital, which is 22 minutes away, I wanted to jump out of the truck because the pain was so intense. I had never understood why someone would want to die or commit suicide, but I started to then. **I just wanted the pain to go away.** When we arrived at the hospital, I was given a dose of IV Dilaudid, a very powerful narcotic pain killer. It did nothing. Thirty minutes later another dose. Nothing.

I was writhing in such extreme pain that I was calling out to God, rocking back and forth, and crying, begging Him to stop the pain. I asked for a third dose, and that was when the doctor pulled my wife aside. He expressed to her that he could not give another dose and was concerned that my tolerance was so high. This is code for, "I think your husband is drug seeking."

I honestly did not think things could get any worse, but clearly, they had. My wife, dumbfounded, just looked at him because she knew I had never used a single drug in my life. I don't even drink – nothing. At this point, even she was shaking her head.

She decided to text our church family for prayer. It just so happens that my primary care physician receives those texts, and he called the hospital. He spoke with the ED physician and assured him that I was not a drug abuser. The problem was that the ER doc had no idea what to do to treat me. I have since learned and realized that doctors are not God. They truly don't know everything, and sometimes, they are just as frustrated and confused as the patient.

We should not put such expectations on them. It truly is unfair, but they were my only hope for relief. And there was no relief. I wanted my life to end. That is extremely hard for me to say, but it is true. I wanted out of pain so bad, I didn't care about anything else. I just wanted the pain to stop. I have two small children, but they never entered my mind. The pain was too intense. There were no thoughts about how would my wife do without me. Nothing. I could not think of anything other than begging God to make the pain stop. I believe now that this is the reason why some people commit suicide. It's not that they want to die; it's that they want the pain to stop.

When the doctor came back into the room, I begged him for a muscle relaxer. He asked why, and I told him I had no idea. I just knew it was like I had a charley horse all over my body, but it was relentless in my upper back. He agreed, probably seeing no harm in it, and the nurse put the medicine via syringe into my IV. I watched it go in while continuing my rocking motion, trying to find any relief possible. Within ten seconds, my muscle spasms ceased, and the pain went away. The doctor looked at me and asked, "What just happened?"

I replied, "I have no idea. You're the doctor. You tell me."

About two hours later my MRI results came back, and one of the admitting hospitalists came to speak with me. The intent was to have me admitted for high dose IV steroid treatment. He sat me down, told me he had reviewed my MRI, reviewed the notes from the admission at the military hospital, and actually apologized for the poor treatment that I received there. God bless him.

I laughed. "Yeah, Doc, I know." He went on to say I had a spinal cord lesion nearly 3 cm long at the C2–C3 vertebrae, and this was what was causing my symptoms. He showed my wife and me the film. He wanted me admitted. However, I had an appointment with my outpatient neurologist, who is extremely busy but was willing to make an exception given my circumstances. I did not want to miss this appointment, and he understood this.

Finally, we had an answer. To be honest, all I could think was, *If the Air Force will do this to me, after all I've done and accomplished, who else would they do it to?*

I did not want anyone to have to experience anything like what I had, especially after serving their country. And I was intent on doing whatever I could to ensure it didn't happen again.

CHAPTER 30: COMBAT HOSPITAL

One of the strangest situations happened when I arrived home. I had had enough of Kandahar, enough of military medicine, and enough of triggers. I just wanted to relax. I was both mentally and physically exhausted by my whole experience. I needed time to recoup, or at least as much as I could with my body not responding correctly.

I decided to use television as a distraction, a way of numbing myself, a way of escape. Incidentally, numbing is a PTSD symptom. I wanted to watch something so I could stop thinking about things for a while. I remembered my sweet grandmother watching soap operas when I was a kid, and now here I was, much older, almost incapacitated, sitting with a blanket, watching TV.

When I ate, I had to use a special foam tool that attaches to the end of a fork because I couldn't hold onto things due to the nerve damage that affected my fine motor skills. Otherwise, I would simply drop both the fork and whatever else I had on it. This was a kind gesture from my occupational therapist who understood the challenges I was confronting.

As I sat there, all I could think of was, *How did my life come to this?* I often ask combat veterans if they ever thought they would end up where they are now, and inevitably, they say no. So, there I was in front of the TV with my blanket and foam-wrapped fork, trying not to spill my food or hit the side of my face and stab myself. I refused to watch soap operas; my life was a soap opera enough.

My mother-in-law had moved in to help us for the three months of my recovery. She was a godsend and helped me with our two boys who had a hard time seeing their dad who could barely walk or give them a hug. When I had returned home, I promised Joshua that I would go outside and play football with him. As I could barely stand up, I went outside, grabbed the football as best I could and tried my hardest to throw it to him, all to no avail. This was the moment I had prayed for in Afghanistan. To make it home alive and to once again be able to play football with my son. It was one of the motivations that kept me going through many grueling days and nights. When all of the other Air Force officers got killed in Kabul, this was the moment I was looking forward to the most. It would have meant that I had survived. Unfortunately, survival doesn't mean escape from harm completely.

Due to my spinal cord issues, I knew this wasn't going to be exactly the way I had planned it for almost a year. Instead of the strength of a 5'10'' 195 lb. man, it was more like a man throwing who had Parkinson's disease. The ball flopped out of my hand and onto the ground only a few inches from where I threw it. I knelt down, grabbed it again and threw it with everything I had. It went two feet this time. My 6-year-old son ran from about 12 feet away, looked up at me from where he picked up the ball, handed it to me and said, "It's okay, Daddy. I'm just glad you are home alive." I will never forget that look on his precious little face as he tried to console me while tears ran down my face. I felt like I had failed. I felt as if my son had asked for only one thing, and I couldn't give it to him.

The next day, I was at home on the couch as my mother-in-law had left to go shopping. As I flipped through the channels in a mindless manner, there it was a show I could never have imagined seeing on TV. A show about a hospital – but not just any hospital, a *ROLE 3* hospital. Not only that, but a ROLE 3 hospital in Kandahar, Afghanistan. THIS WAS OUR HOSPITAL! What in the world? A show about what it's like at a ROLE 3 hospital in a war zone, in Kandahar, in Afghanistan. It was based on the Canadians' experience – who had left just before the Americans took over – manning the ROLE 3. What were the chances of that happening? Here I was trying to get away from everything possible to think about my war experience, and it was right in front of me. I quit. Well, I turned it off.

Then I just sat there. It was very quiet in the house. I couldn't exercise. I could barely walk. I couldn't go to work. I couldn't eat very well. I was basically an invalid. I began to pray and then sighed. There was this show that I desperately wanted to get away from and yet wanted to watch. I could no longer contain my curiosity. I succumbed to its calling . . . just to see what it was like.

I sat there, reliving and reexperiencing more thoughts, feelings, and emotions than you can imagine. The life I had lived and experienced was playing out right in front of me. They even got the sign correct that said Kandahar Airfield. It was an exact replica. Oh, the people were different, but it was the same place, same issues, same injuries. I just sat there mesmerized by what I was seeing.

You see, when you come out of a theater of war, you either want to get completely away from everything that reminds of you what you experienced out of fear of there being a triggering event, or you can't stay away from it. You are like a moth drawn to a light, only to find you are endangering yourself by coming too close. And just how close is safe?

Sometimes I got angry watching it, sometimes I cried, sometimes I flashed back to the experience of it all. But I could not *not* watch. I had to. There was just something about wanting to "get it right" and honestly, they didn't. There were so many things they showed that happened that didn't happen. Sensationalism for TV, I'm sure. But this experience of deciding to watch or not watch television with all of its triggers is very much what it's like for combat veterans who come home. We are afraid of the triggers, but we are drawn to them.

In my first book, I wrote about adrenaline and high-risk behaviors. You know you shouldn't engage in high-risk behaviors like bungee jumping or driving fast, but you want to feel the intense "aliveness" you had in theater. This is why a lot of combat veterans get themselves into trouble. We don't like the mundane. We want high power, high intensity life-and-death living. Sitting on the couch, hurting, is nothing like that. So, we engage in whatever high-risk behaviors we can to feel alive. I know it's not healthy, but it's what we do.

My wife confronted me about this behavior, much the same way many in your family might. In essence, she said, "You just can't stop, can you? You just cannot relax. You always have to be doing something." This said a lot. I imagine my behavior was akin to that of someone on a drug high. Once you feel the high, you don't want to lose it. As an example, I've been up since 1:30 a.m. writing. I just can't seem to shut it off.

I finished the *Combat Hospital* series and relived and reexperienced more than I wanted. Thank God there was only one season. At least my curiosity was resolved. Resolution is what we are after, even if we don't know it. We need resolution with people who died, with why we were there, with the experiences we cannot forget. We desperately need resolution and resiliency. I have no idea which one comes first. Maybe you are smarter than I. I just know we need both.

CHAPTER 31: VETERANS PREFERENCE – NOT IN THE VA!

Timeline: Approximately 2 months post deployment.

After I had returned home and experienced the "unwelcome home," it became clear I needed to find a new job. You would think that a psychologist with military and combat experience would be a prime candidate for a job in the VA system. Even I didn't see this coming. The irony of all ironies was now upon me. Who would ever have thought that when working for the Department of Veterans Affairs, you actually lose your veteran's preference when it comes to applying for another job if you already work for them?

When applying for another VA position within the VA, I'm considered an internal candidate. Sounds like that would be a plus, right? Turns out not so much. In reality, even though I am currently considered a disabled veteran, and have earned a 10-point veteran's preference, I lose any benefit once I am already in the VA system. So, all of my service, sacrifice, and willingness to die for country was now delegated down to that equal to any other internal VA employee who may or may not have sacrificed for our country. What was even more upsetting than finding this out was the attitude of the VA human resource specialist who basically blamed me for thinking that I deserved something more because I had served my country. In essence, this is what I was told, "Do you think you are more valuable as an employee just because you served in a war zone? I have just as much experience as you do, and I shouldn't be penalized just because I didn't join the military."

Are you kidding me? First of all, yes, I believe when you raise your hand to volunteer to sacrifice and possibly die to serve this country there should be benefits for doing so. Isn't that the whole point of veteran's preference in the first place? Then to be shamed into thinking I am asking for more than I have earned (not deserved) is a sad state of affairs. To confirm that I didn't have this veteran preference complex in which I felt I "deserved" more than the next person, I checked out my thinking with a few VA folks who have served 25 plus years.

Their answer: if you served in the military and suffered a disability from your service, then yes, you did earn it, and you should maintain your veteran's preference. Yet again, the government's logic regarding veterans was appalling. Of all places, you would think that the Department of Veterans Affairs would be the one place where I could actually apply veteran's preference and have it count for something.

CHAPTER 32: "I'M SORRY, SIR, BUT YOU CAN'T VOTE. YOU DIDN'T SEND BACK YOUR VOTER REGISTRATION CARD."

Honestly, I was taken aback, or maybe a better word is "stunned" to hear someone say that to me after I had just returned from Afghanistan and was now at our local polling place. I blinked a few times, trying to grasp what was happening. I slightly shook my head. "Are you being serious?" I asked. The response, "Unfortunately, sir, I am. You didn't mail back your voter registration card."

I stood there, looking around in disbelief that this was really happening. There were a lot of people bustling around and people giving them directions on how to actually use the voting machines.

So, I thought to myself, *I leave to serve our country, a place where we fight and risk our lives for the freedom of others to have a right to vote. And here I am, unable to do that which I have risked my life to ensure? I must be on camera.* Seriously, this could not be happening. This was a joke, and someone was going to jump out and say "surprise." But that never happened.

"There must be an exception for those of us who are in the military, correct?" I asked. "Oh, you are in the military," he responded in an upbeat manner, which gave me a glimmer of hope. All I could think was that someone would be able to easily fix this red tape issue. "That's awesome. Thank you for your service," he stated, and I was even more hopeful. But then it's like that recording you get on your phone that would beep and say, "I'm sorry, the number you have dialed has been disconnected and no longer in service. Please try your call again." I felt trying to resolve this issue was futile. I was going to get the same response no matter what I tried. It was as if I had dialed a wrong number and kept doing it over and over and over. Eventually, you quit trying.

He repeated, "I'm sorry, sir. Without a valid registration, you can't vote."

"Ugh," I grunted. My shoulders shrank down. "Heavy sigh" as my friend Dr. AJ Williams would say. The gentleman then stated empathically, "I truly am sorry. I wish there was something I could do. I feel really bad about this."

I just shook my head slowly as the weight of my deployment ran through my head like a high-speed HD video. *What is the purpose, what is this all for*, I thought. The sacrifice, the service, the bodies of all of our military members who got killed or severely injured so that we have freedom in this country and a right to vote. I remembered seeing on television the Iraqi people with their purple thumbs, indicating they had voted, proud of being able to show it off for the very first time. But here I was, back in the US, my own country, my own state, even in my own city – China Spring, Texas – but I was not being allowed to vote.

I didn't want to make a scene. I knew it wasn't this gentleman's fault. It was the government, trying to ensure voter integrity. I get that, but seriously, me of all people? Where is the logic, the clarity of thought? Where is BG Kendall, the Commander of Kandahar Airfield, my boss who with one statement or stroke of his pen could fix things immediately? Literally, I stood there trying not to get angry and thinking to myself once again, *Nobody will believe this. You can't make this stuff up.*

I sighed one final time and said "thank you" for at least trying to help, as he had called someone in higher headquarters in Waco to try to rectify the situation to no avail.

I left that day feeling deflated. As if my life didn't matter. If I had just not volunteered, I could have easily voted. How in the world is this even possible? Seriously, military members who serve overseas and come home can't vote? This must be an anomaly. It must be. But then I'm beginning to think that with everything else that's happened since I went on deployment, this is just par for the course. Deep, heavy sigh!

Serving one's country takes sacrifice, but to be honest, I never imagined in my wildest dreams one of those sacrifices would be to not have the opportunity to vote. I mean with all of the voter fraud that we hear about, am I one of those guys? No way! I fight for the exact opposite. And yet here I am. Just like in the airport with TSA when they begin to question me and pull me aside. Geeze, people, I have an active duty military ID, I'm a Lieutenant Colonel for God's sake. I went to Afghanistan to fight against terrorism, and you think I have to be double checked before I get onto a flight? I'm not even carrying a weapon.

"Sure, I'll take off my shoes." As I look at them directly in the eye, I say to myself, *Don't make an issue out of this David, it isn't worth it.* Most people have no idea how many times veterans have to use their inhibitory skills. We have so many things we would love to say, but if we do, we know what will happen. People will think we are just angry veterans. So, most of us say nothing and keep it inside. But trust me, if you only knew.

Literally, I sometimes think that veterans upon return to the US feel that this is all surreal. And sometimes I wonder if it's experiences like these that create the shift from flashbacks to traits of dissociation. The surreal-ness of it all sure makes sense at times. It's easier to mentally check-out than it is to try to solve yet another conflicting belief system. So, if you see your loved one with that thousand-yard stare, there is probably a good reason for it. They are literally lost in their head, reliving visual experiences and feeling hopeless in trying to change a system. In the military, we are the enforcers. If something isn't right, we fix it. We come back home, and it's out of our hands. Someone else has to fix it, and honestly, a lot of times, it doesn't get fixed. And this leads to more irritability and anger. In theater, we are used to getting our way through aggression. But clearly, that is not a good idea in this context. I could escalate, but what good would it do?

I left and went home, just thinking about what had transpired. I'm not even sure how I got home. I think I was on autopilot in my head. I just kept shaking my head, thinking how crazy this was. I was hoping I would awaken from a bad dream but, alas, it was real.

CHAPTER 33: WHAT YOU ARE EXPERIENCING IS A NORMAL REACTION TO AN ABNORMAL SITUATION

The military, or at least those in the military mental health arena, have a saying which goes, "What you are experiencing is a normal reaction to an abnormal situation." I've heard it time and time again, but it didn't make a lot of sense until I came back from war. Of course, I'm normal, what's wrong with you?

I was in Montgomery, Alabama, with my wife and two sons to celebrate my wife's completion of Commissioned Officer Training and entry into the military. For my wife to join the Air Force was a total shock to me. She is not what I think of when I think of military, but, boy, was I very, very wrong. She is going to make a great officer in the US Air Force. To celebrate, we went to Texas Roadhouse for lunch.

Over lunch, we talked about her experiences to date in the military. She hated boot camp, but had now graduated and was done with it. Like me, Katherine has high expectations of herself. In this way, we are not normal. We are two very high anxiety, Type A, high risk, high reward people. It was definitely harder than what she had expected. I am so proud of her and her willingness to sacrifice for our country. She is truly amazing, smart, and beautiful. I'm not the least biased, because it's all true.

We were discussing her experiences and how she has to wear her hair in a bun and how she does not enjoy the Air Force uniform. Apparently, they are not made to be flattering. She talked about the sleepless nights, the intense workouts, the yelling, all of it. Yet, she was proud. Proud that she made it, and proud she can do 40 pushups in 60 seconds (22 more than she could do when she arrived).

Suddenly, I heard this sound, a very special and distinct sound I had heard many times before. In the time it takes to blink, I hit the deck right there in the Texas Roadhouse. I was lying on the floor and started to cover my head when it hit me; that sound was the alarm for a rocket attack. It was the same alarm sound we used in Kandahar. But I wasn't at war. I was in Alabama, not Afghanistan. What just happened?

I did what I was trained to do. I reacted in a way that could save my life from a rocket attack and shrapnel. Except at that moment I was not in Kandahar. I was in a prone position on the floor at Texas Roadhouse in Montgomery, Alabama, surrounded by peanuts and who knows what else and had a room full of people staring at me. No rocket attacks here, but for me, the sound I heard was (and is) paired through classical conditioning to hit the ground.

I have done this hundreds of times before. When I hear the sound, I hit the ground. Sound, ground, sound, ground, sound, ground. This is normal for me and everyone else who has been to war, or at least at an FOB where early detection measures have been implemented. But I wasn't in a war; I was home. Someone needed to tell my body and mind that information.

So, I got up, dusted the peanuts off, and looked around at everyone staring at me. I smiled and sat back down. My lovely wife held my hand and asked if I was okay. I said I was fine.

"What just happened?" she asked. Silence on my part. She waited a few moments and asked, "Do you want to talk about it?"

"Not really," I responded while shaking my head. I sat there and realized that I had changed. I was no longer the same person. I was embarrassed and wanted to cry, but I refused. I knew something was wrong, but I didn't even realize it until the trigger of the alarm. As I sat there with my thoughts and my feeble attempt to suppress my feelings, I felt very much alone. My eyes were tearing up, but I stopped it with great effort. All I could think was that it isn't normal for everyone else; they didn't just react and hit the floor. They didn't think twice about that sound. That is when I began to wonder, "Am I normal?"

I thought back on what I had been taught. What I was experiencing was a "normal reaction, to an abnormal situation." Welcome to the world of post-war zone behavioral training. This was going to take a while. My heart finally stopped pounding, and, thankfully, I didn't start sweating. I was embarrassed enough without that.

The question I pondered was how long was this going to take to unlearn. As a psychologist, I like to think I'm the normal one, and everyone else is crazy. I say that jokingly. But in reality, I do believe I'm normal. A normal guy from a small town called Oakwood, Illinois. And yet, I was the only one on the floor. That was not normal. My civilian reality had just met my military reality. I wondered how long it would take to "change back." The problem seemed obvious.

The military does an amazing job of up-training its warriors. What it doesn't do is adequately down-train us.

Here's the other problem – you don't change back.

In so many ways, this was my new normal. I have a very different baseline now, especially in regards to how I see the world. I feel torn between whether or not I want to live in this new world in which I feel more prepared to deal with threats, or in the old world of my pre-military baseline, in a state which some would call "obliviousness" to the threats of this world. It's like the difference between addressing this world as a protected child or as the protecting adult.

In some ways, I don't want it to go back. I want to be ready, to be prepared. That is the Boy Scout motto after all. I had so many thoughts, so many challenges related to trying to get back to who I was. My two worlds were colliding, and I didn't want them to. I think half the reason people don't talk about what happens in a war zone is because they don't want to *adulterate* what they have back at home. We want to keep it separate. If these two realities collide, it defies the notion of leaving war there and peace here. Assuming we can mitigate terrorism to OCONUS.

Many warriors do not talk about their experiences of war because they do not want to adulterate their world. If we do share, then those we care about may suffer, even if to a lesser degree, the thoughts we have in our head. We have no desire for others to suffer as we do.

This is a conflict many returning soldiers deal with, and it is why people exhibit some unhealthy behaviors when they come home. Trying to deal with this new baseline and reality is difficult (especially when you discover it on the floor of a Texas Roadhouse). People can't sleep, so they drink or take over the counter or illicit drugs. People need to feel safe, so they buy weapons and cameras and guard dogs. People need to keep that adrenaline rush they had in war, so they buy motorcycles, bungee jump, and exhibit high risk behavior. Sometimes they refuse to watch the news or TV in general because it's simply too hard to watch. The news is constantly about killing or stabbing or fire, etc. Others do the opposite and find themselves engulfed in world events. People do a lot of things to try to bring homeostasis (normalcy) back into their lives. Does this sound familiar?

CHAPTER 34: YOU CAN'T SPEAK AT THE WOUNDED WARRIOR CONFERENCE BECAUSE, WELL . . . YOU GOT WOUNDED IN AFGHANISTAN. WHAT?

Timeline: Almost a year and a half since returning to the United States

Although I had been in contact with my lawyer from the Air Force's Area Defense Counsel regarding my MEB, I was constantly reminding myself to think what this is like for people who are of lower rank or may suffer from a mTBI, depression, significant PTSD symptoms, etc. I can only imagine how it would probably have been; it was definitely frustrating for me. All this time, I was not allowed to be on orders or get paid. I was still on Code 37, awaiting a response from headquarters stating I either was or was not physically fit for the Air Force.

Three years prior, I had been a speaker at the Air Force Wounded Warrior conference. In 2015, I received a call to give another talk about what it was like to deploy to a war zone because they enjoyed my previous presentation so much, or so they said. I was happy to oblige. The issue was that to have my travel paid for, I would have to be on orders. Remember, due to the MEB, I was on code 37 (no pay, no points), so I could not teach at the Air Force Wounded Warrior conference because, well . . . I was a wounded warrior.

This didn't make a lot of sense to me. I sought a waiver through the process and was denied. So, there I was, a seasoned speaker who was injured while serving my country, and I couldn't speak at a conference with wounded warriors about what it's like to go to war because I'd gone to war and been wounded. You can't make this stuff up!

CHAPTER 35: TWO YEARS LATER. LT COL THARP, YOU OWE US $291.81

Timeline: Almost two years after returning home from Kandahar

I received a message saying that I owed the US Air Force $291.81 for not returning my M-16. It is at times like this when you know who your friends are and who you can count on. I first tried to solve the problem myself, even going so far as to make a telephone call back to Kandahar in the off chance my weapon was still there. Yes, I said it. Cold calling Kandahar airfield to see if they happened to have a missing weapon since they were the ones who took it prior to my medevac flight. Remember the previously mentioned situation with the Georgians and weapons? Well, once again, even flying out of Afghanistan, we were not allowed to have weapons with us.

I finally found a solution in Col (Ret) Thomas Berry at the Air Force Academy. I am proud to know him as a friend and colleague. Below was his message in response to my quandary. The receiving name to which the email was sent, has been changed.

From: Berry, Thomas J Jr Civ USAF USAFA USAFA/CWC
Sent: Thursday, March 21, 2013 11:03 AM
To: JONES, JAMES D USAF USAFA 3 LRS/CL
Subject: RE: Mobility Gear Overdue Turn-In for Dr. Tharp,
Evacuated from Afghanistan

Mr. Jones:

Lt Col Dave Tharp is an AF reserve doctor assigned to USAFA/CW –
the Peak Performance Center (formerly called the Cadet Counseling
Center). Two years ago he volunteered to support the war effort,
and went to Afghanistan as part of the deployed NATO forces.
While in Kandahar he became seriously ill, so ill he was Medevac'd
out of Afghanistan, never to return.

Because of his medical condition (long story we do not need to
cover here), he is currently going thru the Medical Evaluation
Board process, and I anticipate he will be medically separated from
the AF reserves.

The good folks in the 3 LRS/LGRMS are now asking him to return
his canteen cover, web belt, gas mask, poncho, canteen cup, etc.
Total new value of missing gear is under $300. Major item is the
$191 gas mask.

Sir, Lt Col Tharp is ill; he is now at home in Texas – and I suspect
most of the missing items were left in Kandahar when he was
Medevac'd out. I feel confident in saying the MEDEVAC folks were
not too worried about his canteen cup when they sent him to
Germany, then the states, with a potentially life threatening
illness.

Can you use this e-mail or a letter on official letterhead from me –
the Unit Reserve Coordinator in CW – to "write-off" the missing
property, and close this case. Frankly, he has already suffered
enough.

Respectfully
Tom Berry

Thomas J. Berry, Jr.
Deputy Director
Center for Character & Leadership Development

2354 Fairchild Drive, Suite 5A18
USAF Academy, CO 80919

P.S. If we must, we will do a Report of Survey – but in a time of a reduction of civilian manpower by 20%, I frankly would like to by-pass that time-sink.

Dr. Berry is an outstanding servant leader and the Deputy Director of Character & Leadership Development at the Air Force Academy. I cannot thank him enough for bringing clarity of thought to a system that is designed to ensure we have a system in place for gear, but sometimes goes awry. One of the things I love about the military is that reason most often does prevail. Dr. Berry was even willing to go down and buy this equipment personally if it didn't get resolved. These are the kinds of people who reveal their character at times like this.

CHAPTER 36: THE PROCESS OF SYMPTOM UNDERREPORTING AND OVERREPORTING

There is a belief that when warriors leave the military they overreport symptoms so they can receive a higher disability rating from the Veterans Benefit Board (VBA). The higher the disability rating, the more money a service member receives from the government. I would presume that this is a true statement for some, but most AD/G/R service members underreport their symptoms. Allow me to explain psychologically what I think is actually happening.

When you are in the military, your security clearance and your job can be affected if you admit to certain psychological disorders. President Obama attempted to alleviate this problem by requiring a change to the questions on SF 86 form, part 2, question 21 about whether or not you have experienced a specific mental health issue. But SF 86 still asks, "In the last 7 years, have you consulted with a mental health professional (psychiatrist, psychologist, counselor, etc.) or have you consulted with another health care provider about a mental health related condition?" (YES/NO.) "If you answer 'Yes,' provide the dates of treatment and the name and address of the therapist or doctor below, unless the consultation(s) involved only marital, family or grief counseling, not related to violence by you."

Military members fear they could lose their security clearance, career, livelihood, and more, if they are forthcoming with any information that could put them in a risk category. By risk, I mean anything that would force them to disclose they are on certain psych meds, or have certain diagnoses. Therefore, when you are in the military, you are encouraged to

minimize any symptoms, issues, concerns, and/or diagnoses that could ruin your career.

As a result, even though they may have symptoms related to post-deployment, sexual assault or abuse, childhood issues, previous trauma, depression, etc., there is a tendency for military members to downplay or minimize these issues. It only makes psychological sense. Not only is there still a stigma about mental health, but also the last thing any pilot, nuclear weapons person, or other highly technical field person wants is to be prevented from doing their job. They will NOT disclose any problems that could possibly cause them to alter their career path. In reality, they not only don't disclose, they also do not get treated for many symptoms that could be eliminated. Then the inevitable: they either retire, are removed due to symptomatology, or quit and end up in the VA.

During interviews, these veterans have consistently NOT disclosed information, oftentimes for decades. Now, they can finally get the help they need without fear of reprisal. So, they disclose. The problem is there is no documentation or medical records to substantiate their claims because they underreported. Now because they no longer have to worry about those consequences, they will disclose the truth about what they have been experiencing. Unfortunately, the provider may not believe them, thinking they are trying to "game" the system.

I have a friend who has been deployed four times. He never disclosed that he suffers from symptoms related to PTSD: fear of death, night sweats, hypervigilance, hyperarousal, avoidance, and a few other symptoms. Now that he is out of the military, he has disclosed this information in an attempt to get help. What will the provider do to "validate" that this possible diagnosis occurred as a result of military service? Look for documentation or military records. When he goes to look, they are simply not there. This is even more difficult for people who were in special ops.

The veterans are left trying to answer questions about a specific incident that caused their condition. When I was in Kandahar, I saw death every single day. Am I supposed to single out one particular death that impacted me more than others? It was, in my opinion, cumulative exposure which led to PTSD, but the VA system isn't organized to handle that as an answer. There has to be *one specific incident*, not multiple or cumulative instances. Where does this come from? The influence of the female sexual assault protocols from Cognitive Behavior Therapy and Prolonged Exposure Therapy. But remember, combat trauma is very different, so different in fact that a totally different resource for treating PTSD had to be created. Enter "The Combat PTSD Resiliency Formation Training program." You can find it on our website at ProjectHealingHeroes.org.

When answering questions about the specific incident, you have to have dates, times, names, location, etc. It's very difficult to obtain that information in the heat of battle. When I was confronted with these questions for my PTSD assessment by my provider, I needed to provide one specific example. I tried to explain that it is not just one trauma that often occurs, but that multiple traumatic experiences occur during deployment.

Combat trauma is more than just one incident. It's made up of a deployment's worth of experiences.

This is often very frustrating for veterans to navigate because, again, the current PTSD treatments for military PTSD are based on female sexual assault survivors whose trauma is mostly limited to a singular experience. Combat PTSD is very different. I refused to say that one death was more important than another. I viewed each person as an individual. On the other side of the coin, one person was no more or less valuable than the other. And remember, military personnel risk losing their security clearance if they disclose the fact that they have sought mental health treatment. This is the type of quandary we put our warriors in. My VA provider was shocked and said, "I thought the President took those requirements out."

"Well, if he had, why were they still on the VA form?" was my response.

There are other examples, but the point is veterans, as compared to current military members, for the most part do not over-exaggerate their symptoms. For purposes of clarity, I define the term "veteran" here to describe someone who is no longer in the military. Instead, they are finally able to be forthcoming and feel free to be honest without fear of losing their jobs, their clearance, or their livelihoods. Yet we are told on many occasions that those folks are gaming the system. I just shake my head back and forth at those who have no idea what is really going on.

At one point, over 80% of the VA employees were former military. It is now less than 40%. It's no wonder why the providers don't understand either military culture or what we go through to fight for this country. It's sometimes another battle once we come home.

CHAPTER 37: TAKE THE 30% DISABILITY OR RISK LOSING BOTH YOUR RETIREMENT AND DISABILITY

Timeline: Almost 2.5 years post deployment

MEDICAL EVALUATION BOARDS

It was now time for my MEB to determine if I was still fit for duty.

As mentioned before, after a soldier is hurt, it is policy that the Air Force will put the soldier on a Code 37 (no pay, no points) until it determines fitness for duty. So, after two and a half years of waiting for the Air Force to make a decision, it came back with an offer of immediate retirement with 30%permanent disability. I wanted to remain in the Air Force and felt that I could continue contributing to the mission. Not surprising, the 30% disability is the lowest percentage that the Air Force could give me with my current medical issues. I had been talking with the Air Force lawyers, and they indicated that I could challenge the 30% but possibly risk losing everything, or I could take the 30% permanent disability and retire.

After winning the 2012 Air Force Association VA Employee of the Year Award, I honestly felt very frustrated that the Air Force wanted me to retire. Here I am with this vast experience, freshly back from completing a significant NATO role in a theater of war, and they are basically done with me. My heart was in the Air Force to serve, not to retire. It was then that I went to San Antonio to talk with my lawyer about how to proceed. Funny thing was, he indicated I wouldn't even have to show up for the MEB because I had proven my case. He could submit the paperwork for the MEB waiver which would grant me the opportunity to stay in the Air Force and all *should* go well. But honestly, I wanted to look these folks in the eye, explain what a nightmare the Integrated Disability Evaluation System (DES)[12] system had been, how we seriously needed to look at how we were treating our returning war veterans – especially those with injuries – and to make changes. Do you get the feeling I never learn how futile this process is?

After I arrived at my appointed time on the appointed day, I was told that my lawyer was "unavailable." What they really meant was that he was TDY (Temporary Duty), aka: GONE. Why was I just hearing about this? One and a half years of strategy with my lawyer, and now he just happened to be gone. Why hadn't he told me?

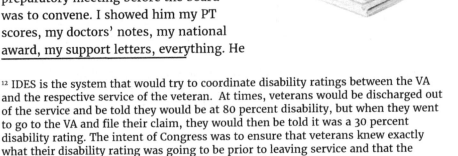

The board decided to give me more time to meet with another attorney. Two days later, I was re-assigned to another lawyer. He reviewed my case, I was called in, and we sat down and had a preparatory meeting before the board was to convene. I showed him my PT scores, my doctors' notes, my national award, my support letters, everything. He

---

[12] IDES is the system that would try to coordinate disability ratings between the VA and the respective service of the veteran. At times, veterans would be discharged out of the service and be told they would be at 80 percent disability, but when they went to go to the VA and file their claim, they would then be told it was a 30 percent disability rating. The intent of Congress was to ensure that veterans knew exactly what their disability rating was going to be prior to leaving service and that the agencies would coordinate effort and ensure they were on the same page.

finally looked up, interlaced his fingers together, leaned back in his chair, and said, "Well, Major Tharp, I've reviewed all your documents. There is some good news and some bad news. Which do you want first?"

"I'll take the good news first, actually," I replied.

"Okay. Well, everything is impressive, and I believe you will do well at the board hearing."

"And the bad news?"

"You will win the battle and lose the war."

Now he had my attention. "What did that mean?" I asked him.

"Well," he said. "You can win your argument here before the board. Your credentials are stellar, the documents are thorough. You can even argue you are as healthy as you were before you had your injury. That being said, you still cannot win. If you get reinstated, what will you accomplish?"

I was totally taken back by his question. For a year and a half, I had made the argument that I was healthy, and now I was being told that I would win but lose. At the time I didn't understand exactly what he meant by that, but I do now. I thought his statement was directed solely at me, but then he pointed to a stack of folders. "See those? Those are all active duty men and women with 17 or 18 years in service. They have no guarantees without taking the disability." He continued, "As for you, on one hand you have a 30% disability guaranteed. You can walk away, no questions asked, and we'll pay you each month. That's the win. On the other hand, how supportive has your HQ been?"

I said, "Great, up until I got injured."

"And when was the last time they actually talked with you?"

"About a year ago," I said.

"And how many years of service do you have in?" he asked.

"Eight, well, make that seven as I lost a year being on code 37."

"And you are how old?"

"Forty-seven."

"So that gives you 13 years to get 13 good years in before your mandatory retirement date. Do you think you will be allowed to deploy again?" he asked.

"I highly doubt it."

"So, there is no guarantee you will get 13 good years in. You've already lost one year, HQ hasn't spoken with you in a year, you are non-deployable, and there is no guarantee they will use you in the future. Do I understand that correctly?"

I dislike what lawyers have to do.

When I went to billeting, I think I was still in shock. I was weighing out all the lawyer had said, and this information was heavy on my mind. I saw an LTC who seemed a bit distraught. Because I'm a psychologist, it's in my nature to ask. He shared with me that he was here for the MEB, and I quickly did something I don't normally do. I finished his sentence, "And they are forcing you to decide between your disability rating versus not having a guaranteed retirement." He looked surprised – how in the world could I know that?

"Exactly" he said. "My wife has been praying about this situation and crying all day, and we came here with a firm confidence that I was going to be able to stay in. But I cannot risk losing my retirement. What other choice do I have? I cannot believe I've been in the military for 17 years, and I will be forced out."

This made my heart sink. Here was a man who had devoted his whole career to serving the military, and this was the offer he was given. Either take 30% or risk losing everything. I cannot imagine too many people who don't take the guaranteed offer. To do otherwise is a huge risk, and we have been taught as military members to mitigate risk at all cost.

Instead of "rolling the dice," I counted on Air Force integrity. Because 30% was the lowest possible disability rating, and because we finally found the source of my spinal illness issues, I felt the Air Force would do the right thing, increase my percentage, and medically discharge me.

It seemed I, like a lot of other veterans, thought the military was going to do the right thing. The Secretary of the Air Force (SECAF), the same person with whom I had my picture taken two months earlier after winning the 2012 Air Force Association Veterans Administration Employee of the Year Award, had a staff that didn't seem to think quite the way I did.

Instead of granting a higher percentage, they did the opposite. They not only took the offer of permanent disability off the table, but they also placed me on TDRL (Temporary Disabled Retirement List). This would force me, for the next 18 months to 2 years in the Air Force Reserve, to go on a no-pay, no-point status, not receive any disability check, but to literally be in a holding pattern. So now not only would it be three years post deployment before I received a disability check, but the Air Force would no longer have me be a part of the mission. To make matters worse, there was now no way to retire. They made it impossible for me to retire given the code 37 and by making the process draw out for 3-4 years. Heartbreak, anger, frustration and disgust are just a few of the emotions I had in my head and heart at that point.

This is what happens when you ask for reconsideration and for people to do the right thing.

CHAPTER 38: DAVID, WAKE UP. I THINK THE HOUSE IS ON FIRE.

Timeline: 3 years post deployment.

If you've ever wondered if things can go from bad to worse, the answer is "yes."

When you come back from deployment, you often wonder if things will ever get back to normal. Unfortunately, reality can sometimes make your transition back to normal challenging. Let's call it just another opportunity to find out how much resilience you really have. There is a reason we called our first book on PTSD *Resiliency Formation Training*.

My wife was studying one evening, and the boys and I were asleep at 2300 (make that 11:00 p.m.). She often stayed up late while she was in medical school. I often worked late into the night when I worked on the house, and Katherine had made a rule that I was not allowed to use power tools after 2:00 a.m. So initially, she didn't think too much about the crackling noises in the living room, but when they didn't stop after a while, she decided to see what was going on. I think it was because she didn't want me to wake up the boys. What she discovered was smoke pouring out of the ceiling vents. She ran upstairs where the boys and I were sleeping. Frantic, she shook me awake. "David, wake up. I think the house is on fire!"

I was in a deep sleep because I often would arouse around 2:00 am, and I don't get much sleep. After realizing the house was on fire, my youngest son did what he was trained to do. He ran to our neighbors about 500 yards away. He actually sprinted, and we couldn't find him at first. My oldest had no desire to even get out of bed, said, "It's not time for school," and fell back asleep. My wife made sure he woke up, and got him out of the house. I tried to put the fire out, but that was a losing effort. My wife told me later that because I wouldn't give up fighting the fire, she threatened to divorce me if I didn't get out of the house. I was so focused on trying to put it out, I lost situational awareness.

In the end, the firefighters couldn't get into the subdivision because they didn't have a key or the code, so by the time they arrived, the house was in flames. The firemen arrived and worked diligently to get the fire under control. The flames had made it up about 30 feet in the air inside the house and were in the attic. At that point, the fire chief felt it was unsafe and called everyone out of the house. It was his call. Our house would go up in flames. We later found out that the firemen were right at the hot spot and gave it one last shot of water. They worked diligently and were able to get the fire under control at the very last minute. Had they walked away, the house would have been a total loss. Thank God for firefighters.

We ended up having to rebuild one-third of our house and spent ten months in a very small hotel room and another eight months in a rental unit. But in the end, we finally were able to get back into our home after the fire, which had started in our wood burning fireplace when a cinder had escaped the flue and caught the roof on fire. Needless to say, we decided it was best during our renovation to replace it with a gas fireplace. At least this way, if something went wrong, we would blow up instead of burn up.

All of these experiences are considered nodal points which tax your resiliency. Some people excel during these times, but for others it can be their last straw.

Some people's lives are like one of the beautiful covered bridges I often saw in Indiana. The problem is that the bridges are not designed to carry significant weight. When a person comes back from deployment, their load bearing capabilities are diminished. It's as if they are a bridge that already has two semis sitting on it, ready to cross. One has to be careful about taking on more difficulties in life, especially when you have a choice.

In therapy, I illustrate that there is a significant amount of energy that you will expend if you take it seriously. Internal stress with PTSD is difficult enough to deal with. If there are significant external stressors, they add even more load and challenge. The best way to deal with internal stress is to completely eliminate or reduce external stress to the best of your best ability. If you do not, the chances of addressing your internal stress are significantly reduced.

If you are interested in reading more about how to treat PTSD, go to our website at ProjectHealingHeroes.org. There you can receive our books on how to treat PTSD.

CHAPTER 39: WE ARE NOT THE REAL HEROES.

Not one of us feels like a hero. I've never met a combat veteran who felt as if they had achieved this status. Actually, we feel very much the opposite. We feel as if we could have done more. We often feel as if we should not have left the war zone as our buddies are still fighting, and there is unfinished business. The problem with our current war is that there never seems to be closure. It's as if you are in a sport and sitting on the bench while watching others play.

It's finally your turn, you get called up, you play the game, and then you are taken out, but the game is still going. Then you are relegated to watching from the sidelines. Every so often, people may get put back into the game (another deployment), but the game just keeps going with or without you.

Many of us *never* feel as if we did enough, and especially not enough to warrant attention for it. Somehow the Air Force Association, the DAV and our Congressman each received my name and information about what I had accomplished. This chapter is not about winning awards. Actually, it's the exact opposite. There is a strong emotion that comes with these types of things. I suspect it's the same feeling when people thank us for our service. When you compare the sacrifice of life to what you did to earn an award, you simply don't feel worthy. There is nothing about it that compares. Nothing. As a matter

FULFILLING OUR PROMISES
TO THE MEN AND WOMEN WHO SERVED

of fact, it hits you right in the gut when you think about the sacrifice others have made. We often get emotional when we are by ourselves. We don't want people to see our tears, our heartache, our loss and pain. Even as I write this on the back patio of our apartment while they rebuild our house, I am attuned to the slightest sounds. Birds happily chirping, a dog walking around. It's quiet. Somber. A moment of reflection for those I will not see in this lifetime, whose lives were cut short.

Why did I survive in Kandahar when all in the JDOC in Kabul died? Why did others who were on the point of the spear have to perish? What plans does God have for me that I am left remaining? What about the families of those who died? Who comforts them? Awards, in light of this, are meaningless.

And although organizations and people applaud your efforts, you never feel as if you gave enough, sacrificed enough, did enough, no matter how much you did.

I think this illustrates how our baseline changes our perspective. Everything we experience in life post deployment is compared to others, and how they gave the ultimate sacrifice. How can you compare anything to that? You simply can't. Their life is over, and you still have yours. That is why most of us feel unworthy of any honor that we may receive.

I've spoken with my brother Joe who was in Vietnam. I asked his permission to share his story. He was 65 years-old before he ever applied for any disability with the VA. When I pressed him on this issue, he made it clear, "David, I had two friends die in Vietnam. I survived. I told God that if he got me home, I would owe him. The government doesn't owe me, and nothing they do can ever bring them back. I am the one who owes a debt." Now that is selfless sacrifice.

CHAPTER 40: A TRUE AMERICAN HERO: NOT ME!

In 2014, Baylor University honored me at a men's basketball game as part of the Wounded Warrior Project. It truly was an honor to be there. There was another gentleman who had served in Iraq in 2003. We were not alone as we had the blessing of having our families join us. Truthfully, I really just wanted to meet the team and let my boys stand center stage at the game to be honored because I truly believe that the family sacrifices just as much and often times more than the military member during deployment.

So why is it that those of us who are left behind have such a hard time being called a "true American hero"? Because we don't feel it. Point blank, I'm not ego-syntonic (good) with being called a hero. It's because our baseline for how we judge things has changed dramatically. Daren Hidalgo sacrificed everything, including his life. I, on the other hand, am still alive. I am no hero.

There are those folks who have suffered the wounds of war, both invisible and visible, countless people who in previous wars would have otherwise died from their injuries. One of the benefits of working at ROLE 3 is that I got to see miracles happen every day, up close and personal. I witnessed the God given talent of those who can stop the bleeding and get people stabilized and bring about healing for those soldiers who would otherwise have died. These soldiers, sailors, airmen and Marines are the true American heroes. They, along with those who have suffered the "invisible wounds of war" from this conflict, are the true heroes.

I hate IEDs. The havoc they can wreak on the body – including the internal organs and brain – are devastating. The service members who endure these blasts are my American heroes.

For most of us that were willing to go and risk our lives, it's simple: we made it home alive. We are grateful just to be alive. In comparison to those who didn't come back

I said I was fine. I lied.

– and that's the key – we don't feel like heroes. We came home, and we get to move on with our lives. Those in the national and local cemeteries do not. After suffering my spinal cord illness, I walked very slowly down the walkway from the plane when I arrived home. People who knew me before deployment knew my high energy level and high ops tempo. I now walk much slower. I process a little more slowly. I ponder things a lot more. More times than I care to count, I flashback to memories of all I've been through. I lose track of time and situational awareness when I do this. I also see the world through a different set of lenses. I make sure I am prepared at all times. I do what I can to never lose my awareness of situations or people. There are threats out there, and it is my job to mitigate them. My life has been forever changed.

CHAPTER 41: NEW MISSION, END STATE AND FINDING PURPOSE AND MEANING IN LIFE

THE MEANING OF LIFE IS TO FIND YOUR GIFT. THE PURPOSE OF LIFE IS TO GIVE IT AWAY.

— PABLO PICASSO

I truly believe that one of the keys to resiliency and resolution is finding a purpose in life. We all need to feel as if we have a role in this world and a purpose for which we are put on this earth. Some at this point might be aware of a book called *The Purpose Driven Life* by Rick Warren. I think it is an excellent resource for people struggling with what their purpose is in life.

After coming back from Afghanistan, a house fire, failing health, serving my country, all I had endured from the VA and my experience with one particular military medical center, I still knew God was not done with me. He had a purpose and a mission for me. Sometimes I wonder if my wife, who is now a psychiatry resident, wonders if I will ever stop. The answer is "no." Not until I die. I am a firm believer that God has me on this earth for a purpose, and I am going to keep doing what I do until my last breath. I don't hear God in an audible voice telling me what to do. I just pray and move in a direction and He seems to open and close doors. I fully expected to be MED boarded out of the Air Force, and yet here I am, at least for now. I fully expected to struggle significantly with spinal cord issues, and yet my recovery has been remarkable. I fully expected that I would never have children, and yet here they are.

When I work with combat veterans, one of the questions I ask them is about their End State.

I want to know what it is that they want out of life? What is most important to them? What do they value more than anything else? I then ask them to write  those desires down and then make every decision with those things in mind. Unfortunately, it is amazing how many combat veterans have no idea what they truly want or desire. Or they focus on what they cannot have. So, I challenge them. I encourage them. I want them to be clear in their minds about what is truly important. I call them the 5 F's: faith, family, friendships, fellowship and fun.

 But I quickly realized that even working directly with veterans, I could only impact a few at a time. I don't agree with many of the current therapy interventions for combat veterans for the reasons previously stated. And I wanted to get as healthy as I could personally.

So, I took the time that God has given me, and I wrote. Just like I do now. Starting at 2:30 a.m. most days, I think about what veterans tell me and what they need. And some days it's pretty easy because Mr. Ed Schmidt, a former Marine, will call me and tell me about another veteran who is suicidal or in need. I pray about it, and I think critically. I use all of my training and education to draw conclusions that, frankly, for some reason, others do not. I have no idea why this is the case. I see things from a very high level, the 50,000-foot view if you will. But I also know what it's like on the ground. I know what it's like to be in war.

Contrary to many people who write on the subject of trauma who have never truly experienced it, I have. It's forever embedded in my memory. It is inescapable, but it does not define me. I have overcome a lot of the symptoms and challenges that trauma exhibits, but not all. Tonight, as I was editing the book one final time, I heard a moderately loud noise and jumped. My wife looked at me and said, "You still have it, don't you?" Well, I guess I do. I just know how to respond better after the initial startle reflex and rush of adrenaline. It was then I thought back on the incoming rockets, the chaos, my medical response team, BG Kendall, and then back to reality in my nice little, somewhat quiet house.

I have found that when I truly have an answer that works for me, it oftentimes seems to work for others as well. That is why I decided to put what I have experienced into a book so that others could vicariously live "what it's like to go to war." It's not fun. It takes its toll on you emotionally, physically and spiritually. But through resilience via prayer and sheer determination and plausible answers, I am being made whole again. And you and your loved ones can also.

I will never know all of the answers, especially the ones to questions like why certain people die and others are saved. I believe we are all on a journey, and some of us are not home yet. We still have work and life to do. But there are certain things I know beyond a shadow of a doubt. God promised that He would never leave me nor forsake me, and He has not.

So, what does one do when one feels compelled to go to war to not only understand what it's like to experience it, but to try to do whatever one can to help people understand it? I wrote. But it does not end there. I believe we not only have to share what knowledge we have, but must also literally give people a cup of cold water. And in Texas, where it's been over 100 degrees for the past two weeks, that is all I desire when I come in from the heat.

I decided to create a nonprofit that would help others drink from the same cup of cold water. So, Daniel Williams, MD, my wife Katherine Tharp, MD, and I started Project Healing Heroes and CombatPTSD.org.

We've since been blessed with BG Kendall, who has joined us in this great adventure.

I cannot wait to see what God has planned. It is amazing to see what happens when people, even combat veterans, find a mission and purpose for their life. Without it, we are aimless. We cannot afford to be aimless in this world. It will not be kind to you. So, aim well.

Get your new mission in life, and find something you feel passionate about. Do not let anything get in the way of accomplishing your mission. Pray about it, and ask God for wisdom and discernment, and move in a particular direction. I have always found that momentum is key, and if you want something done, give it to a busy person. Why? Because they get things done.

I have heard it said that the hardest part of an exercise program is tying your shoes. You have to get up enough motivation to start there. Are your shoes on? Are they tied? Are you moving in a particular direction? It is much easier to turn a ship or a car that is in motion. My challenge for you is this: as you are reading this book and asking yourself what it might be like to go to war, consider that I believe a deployment of  experiences is the only way you can ever know what it's like. Yet, at the same time, we desperately need people who can come along side us and be there when we are ready to talk about these things.

By your reading this book, *you care*. And that is all we really need to know. The sacrifices we make for war are many.

My brother Joe and I just got off the phone after talking about another concept he wanted me to consider. It's about anxiety, anger and rage. It's about sacrifice and what happens to the psyche when people die for a cause, like at Normandy. But even more importantly, what happens when your friends die to take Mosul or Fallujah and then we give it back? We get so incredibly angry and even rageful that we feel American lives were sacrificed for nothing. We cannot tolerate selfless sacrifice without purpose. We do not want those who have died to have died in vain.

We are alive. For whatever reason, God spared us. We may not know why, but we struggle with this very concept of survivor guilt.

Helping us to find our *new mission* in life and our *end state* is key. These are two terms that most veterans are very familiar with from their time in military, but which they don't necessarily apply to their personal lives. But if these concepts are good enough for the US military to use, it's probably smart for us to consider using them in our personal lives.

Your caring enough to try to understand what we have been through and to help us work through these issues shows your heart. And in my opinion, everything starts with the heart.

What happens in war truly doesn't stay in war.

Dear God, may you use this book to reach even one person who is a spouse, caregiver or professional today. May you use them to help those of us who are hurting and can't speak. May they be given discernment to know what to say, when to say it, and how to say it. May they literally be a cup of cold water to those who are thirsty and need rest. Amen.

If you have found this book to be helpful, please let me know. Even a short email would make my day. You can contact me at DrDTharp@projecthealingheroes.org

ACRONYMS LIST

AD – Active Duty

AMA – Against Medical Advice

AMSUS – American Military Surgeons of the United States

AOR – Area of Responsibility

BG – Brigadier General. This is a one-star General who is at the very top of the rank structure. A four-star General (called General) is at the very top of the hierarchy in rank structure.

BSC – Biomedical Service Corp. Area of expertise includes psychologist, social workers, etc.

CL – Class

COA – Course of Action

COB – Company Operating Base

COMKAF – Commander Kandahar Air Field

CONUS – Continental United States

COP – Combat outpost. This is the post that is the most at risk and furthest away from the "wire," usually a small group of soldiers with very little Force Protection, other than what they do for themselves.

COT – Candidate Officer Training

CWC – Cadet Wing Commander

DFAC – Dining Facility

DOD – Department of Defense

DVBIC – Defense Veterans Brain Injury Center

ECP – Entry Control Point

ENG - Engineer

ENV – Environmental

ENVENG – Environmental Engineer. This person assesses, surveys, coordinates and collaborates with others in regards to the warfighting environment.

FOB – Forward Operating Base

FP – Force Protection

IDES – Integrated Disability Evaluation System

G – Guard (National). The Army Guard is designed for operations inside the United States (CONUS).

IDF – Indirect Fire

IED – Improvised Explosive Device

IMA – Individual Mobilization Augmentee

ISAF – International Security Assistance Force

JDAM – Joint Direct Attack Munition. This is often a 500 or 1,000 lb bomb dropped to destroy whatever it hits.

JDOC – Joint Defense Operations Center

KIA – Killed in Action

LGRMS – Local Government Risk Management Services

LOD – Line of Duty. This is the documentation proving that one was injured while serving in the military.

LRMC – Landstuhl Regional Medical Center

LRS – Long Range Systems

MACE – Military Acute Concussion Evaluation

MEB - Medical Evaluation Board

MEDAD – Medical Advisor. This person advises the commander of any medical issues, oftentimes including number of wounded, KIA, etc.

Medevac – Medical Evacuation

MIRP – Medical Incident Response Prevention

MMV – Mechanical Motor Vehicle

MRAP - Mine-Resistant Ambush Protected vehicle

MST – Military Sexual Trauma

MWR – Morale, Welfare and Recreation

NAMSA – NATO Maintenance and Supply Agency

NATO – National Arms Treaty Organization

OCONUS – Outside Continental United States

PREVMED – Preventative Medicine. This person is proactive in the fight on diseases confronted by military members in field conditions. An example is malaria.

R – Reserve. The Reserve is defined by Title 10 but can be activated (active duty) when needed. Title 10 of the United States Code outlines the role of armed forces in the United States Code. It provides the legal basis for the roles, missions and organization of each of the services as well as the United States Department of Defense.

RC – Regional Command

RCS – Regional Command South

ROE – Rules of Engagement

RPG – Rocket-Propelled Grenade

SECAF – Secretary of the Air Force

SHAPE – Supreme Headquarters Allied Powers Europe

SNRI – Serotonin Norepinephrine Reuptake Inhibitor

SRO – Senior Ranking Officer

SSDI – Social Security Disability Insurance

TBI – Traumatic Brain Injury

TDRL– Temporary Disability Retirement List

TDY – Temporary Duty

TOC – Tactical Operations Center

USAFA – United States Air Force Academy

USAFHQ – United States Air Force Headquarters

UCMJ – Uniform Code of Military Justice. This is the legal code the military turns to when discipline is required, including court-martial, when necessary.

VA – Veterans Affairs

VISN – Veterans Integrated Service Network

VOCO – Verbal Orders of the Commander

XO – Executive Officer. This person reports directly and serves the needs of the commander to whom they are assigned. Rank for an XO is typically an O6 (Colonel) or above.

Dedication

This book is dedicated to Joshua and Peyton Tharp. You have both had to sacrifice while mom and dad, at times, served others. We love you as far as the East is from the West. Or, as you say, "to infinity!" Our prayer is that you, too, will find God's calling in your life and never let anything get in the way of fulfilling it.

To Lt. Daren Hidalgo for his complete and utter selfless sacrifice for our country. The jewels in your crown in heaven will be many. I only pray your family can know how much of an impact you have had on those of us who deployed with you. You are my hero, and you will never be forgotten.

ACKNOWLEDGMENTS

Joseph Tharp, M.A. – for serving in Vietnam and enduring all you have been through to create a safe and secure world.

Carol Sands – Your phone calls every morning are my sunshine and encouragement.

Janey Taylor – a/k/a gre gre. Thank you for being such an incredible grandmother and for always being there when we needed you.

Sarah Kemp – for your countless hours of service to our country through the USO. You and your friends made our hell a little more like home.

Brigadier General Jeffrey B. Kendall, USAF (Ret.) – What an amazing example of integrity, service before self and excellence in everything he does. He truly is one in a million and was an incredible blessing to me as the Commander of Kandahar Airfield.

LTC Thomas Downey – A true friend who provided invaluable, honest feedback as a friend and from a military perspective. Thank you for your service to both God and Country.

Ed "Throat Punch" and Denise Schmidt – Two of the most caring and kind individuals who put veterans and family first.

Robert "Mitch" Norman, M.D. – By far one of the best psychiatrists I have ever worked for and whose insight into the world of mental health is beyond measure

Richard Seim, Ph.D. – One of the most insightfully brilliant men I know. Your editorial comments and ideas were extremely helpful in the creation of this book.

Lt Col Thomas Jordan (Ret.) – A man who literally has been in four wars! Thank you for being my friend and mentor.

Rev. (Dr.) Chris Bennett – A godly man who made more of an impact on my spiritual life than I could ever repay. You believed in me, and I hope I have made you proud.

Kevin and Brian Tharp – You guys will never know how much of an impact you have had on my life in ways you don't even know. Thank you for being my brothers and for all the amazing times we have had together. I wish we were closer in proximity.

And finally:

Joseph C. and Norma L. Tharp – My amazing, awesome parents. Although you will never read this and have left this earth, you created me and made me who I am today. I love you to eternity and will see you there in a few short years. You have given me so much in life, and it came at a high price of selfless sacrifice which can never be repaid. For the countless hours of doing what loving parents do, I just want to make you proud.

Made in the USA
Middletown, DE
10 May 2022

65583461R00106